48th Annual Meeting of the Association for Computational Linguistics 2010 (ACL 2010)

System Demonstrations

Uppsala, Sweden
13 July 2010

ISBN: 978-1-61738-824-8

Printed from e-media with permission by:

Curran Associates, Inc.
57 Morehouse Lane
Red Hook, NY 12571

Some format issues inherent in the e-media version may also appear in this print version.

Printed by Curran Associates, Inc. (2010)

For permission requests, please contact the Association for Computational Linguistics at the address below.

Association for Computational Linguistics
209 N. Eighth Street
Stroudsburg, Pennsylvania 18360

Phone: 1-570-476-8006
Fax: 1-570-476-0860

acl@aclweb.org

Additional copies of this publication are available from:

Curran Associates, Inc.
57 Morehouse Lane
Red Hook, NY 12571 USA
Phone: 845-758-0400
Fax: 845-758-2634
Email: curran@proceedings.com
Web: www.proceedings.com

Introduction

Welcome to the proceedings of the system demonstration session. This volume contains the papers of the system demonstrations presented at the 48th Annual Meeting of the Association for Computational Linguistics, held in Uppsala, Sweden, on July 13 2010.

The system demonstrations program offers the presentation of early research prototypes as well as interesting mature systems. The system demonstration chair and the members of the program committee received 65 submissions, 14 of which were selected for inclusion in the program after review by two members of the program committee.

I would like to thank the members of the program committee for their excellent job in reviewing the submissions and providing their support for teh final decision.

Chair

Sandra Kübler, Indiana University

Program Committee:

Thorsten Brants (Google, USA)
Sabine Buchholz (Toshiba Research Europe, U.K.)
Paul Davis (Motorola, USA)
Thierry Declerck (DFKI, Germany)
Markus Dickinson (Indiana University, USA)
Michael Gasser (Indiana University, USA)
Günther Görz (Universität Erlangen, Germany)
Iryna Gurevych (Technische Universität Darmstadt, Germany)
Ahmed Hassan (University of Michigan, USA)
Julia Hockenmaier (University of Illinois, USA)
Wolfgang Hoeppner (Universität Duisburg, Germany)
Angela Klutsch (Universität Duisburg, Germany)
Yuji Matsumoto (Nara Institute of Science and Technology, Japan)
Emad Mohamed (Indiana University, USA)
Preslav Nakov (National University of Singapore)
Nicolas Nicolov (JD Power and Associates, USA)
Petya Osenova (Bulgarian Academy of Sciences, Bulgaria)
Arzucan Ozgur (University of Michigan, USA)
Vahed Qazvinian (University of Michigan, USA)
Paul Rodrigues (University of Maryland, USA)
Nathan Sanders (Indiana University, USA)
Martin Scholz (Universität Erlangen, Germany)
Kiril Simov (Bulgarian Academy of Sciences, Bulgaria)
Antal van den Bosch (Tilburg University, The Netherlands)
Holger Wunsch (Universität Tübingen, Germany)
Annie Zaenen (Palo Alto Research Center, USA)
Desislava Zhekova (Universität Bremen, Germany)

Additional Reviewers:

Daniel Bär (Technische Universität Darmstadt, Germany)
Georgi Georgiev (Ontotext, Bulgaria)
Niklas Jakob (Technische Universität Darmstadt, Germany)
Jason Kessler (JD Power and Associates, USA)
Michael Matuschek (Technische Universität Darmstadt, Germany)
Bjørn Zenker (Universität Erlangen, Germany)

Table of Contents

Conference Program

Tuesday, July 13, 2010

15:00–17:35 *Grammar Prototyping and Testing with the LinGO Grammar Matrix Customization System*
Emily M. Bender, Scott Drellishak, Antske Fokkens, Michael Wayne Goodman, Daniel P. Mills, Laurie Poulson and Safiyyah Saleem

15:00–17:35 *cdec: A Decoder, Alignment, and Learning Framework for Finite-State and Context-Free Translation Models*
Chris Dyer, Adam Lopez, Juri Ganitkevitch, Jonathan Weese, Ferhan Ture, Phil Blunsom, Hendra Setiawan, Vladimir Eidelman and Philip Resnik

15:00–17:35 *Beetle II: A System for Tutoring and Computational Linguistics Experimentation*
Myroslava O. Dzikovska, Johanna D. Moore, Natalie Steinhauser, Gwendolyn Campbell, Elaine Farrow and Charles B. Callaway

15:00–17:35 *GernEdiT - The GermaNet Editing Tool*
Verena Henrich and Erhard Hinrichs

15:00–17:35 *WebLicht: Web-Based LRT Services for German*
Erhard Hinrichs, Marie Hinrichs and Thomas Zastrow

15:00–17:35 *The S-Space Package: An Open Source Package for Word Space Models*
David Jurgens and Keith Stevens

15:00–17:35 *Talking NPCs in a Virtual Game World*
Tina Klüwer, Peter Adolphs, Feiyu Xu, Hans Uszkoreit and Xiwen Cheng

15:00–17:35 *An Open-Source Package for Recognizing Textual Entailment*
Milen Kouylekov and Matteo Negri

15:00–17:35 *Personalising Speech-To-Speech Translation in the EMIME Project*
Mikko Kurimo, William Byrne, John Dines, Philip N. Garner, Matthew Gibson, Yong Guan, Teemu Hirsimäki, Reima Karhila, Simon King, Hui Liang, Keiichiro Oura, Lakshmi Saheer, Matt Shannon, Sayaki Shiota and Jilei Tian

15:00–17:35 *Hunting for the Black Swan: Risk Mining from Text*
Jochen Leidner and Frank Schilder

15:00–17:35 *Speech-Driven Access to the Deep Web on Mobile Devices*
Taniya Mishra and Srinivas Bangalore

15:00–17:35 *Tools for Multilingual Grammar-Based Translation on the Web*
Aarne Ranta, Krasimir Angelov and Thomas Hallgren

Tuesday, July 13, 2010 (continued)

15:00–17:35 *Demonstration of a Prototype for a Conversational Companion for Reminiscing about Images*
Yorick Wilks, Roberta Catizone, Alexiei Dingli and Weiwei Cheng

15:00–17:35 *It Makes Sense: A Wide-Coverage Word Sense Disambiguation System for Free Text*
Zhi Zhong and Hwee Tou Ng

Grammar Prototyping and Testing with the LinGO Grammar Matrix Customization System

Emily M. Bender, Scott Drellishak, Antske Fokkens, Michael Wayne Goodman, Daniel P. Mills, Laurie Poulson, and Safiyyah Saleem
University of Washington, Seattle, Washington, USA
{ebender, sfd, goodmami, dpmills, lpoulson, ssaleem}@uw.edu,
afokkens@coli.uni-saarland.de

Abstract

This demonstration presents the LinGO Grammar Matrix grammar customization system: a repository of distilled linguistic knowledge and a web-based service which elicits a typological description of a language from the user and yields a customized grammar fragment ready for sustained development into a broad-coverage grammar. We describe the implementation of this repository with an emphasis on how the information is made available to users, including in-browser testing capabilities.

1 Introduction

This demonstration presents the LinGO Grammar Matrix grammar customization system[1] and its functionality for rapidly prototyping grammars. The LinGO Grammar Matrix project (Bender et al., 2002) is situated within the DELPH-IN[2] collaboration and is both a repository of reusable linguistic knowledge and a method of delivering this knowledge to a user in the form of an extensible precision implemented grammar. The stored knowledge includes both a cross-linguistic core grammar and a series of "libraries" containing analyses of cross-linguistically variable phenomena. The core grammar handles basic phrase types, semantic compositionality, and general infrastructure such as the feature geometry, while the current set of libraries includes analyses of word order, person/number/gender, tense/aspect, case, coordination, pro-drop, sentential negation, yes/no questions, and direct-inverse marking, as well as facilities for defining classes (types) of lexical entries and lexical rules which apply to those types. The grammars produced are compatible with both the grammar development tools and the grammar-based applications produced by DELPH-IN. The grammar framework used is Head-driven Phrase Structure Grammar (HPSG) (Pollard and Sag, 1994) and the grammars map bidirectionally between surface strings and semantic representations in the format of Minimal Recursion Semantics (Copestake et al., 2005).

The Grammar Matrix project has three goals—one engineering and two scientific. The engineering goal is to reduce the cost of creating grammars by distilling the solutions developed in existing DELPH-IN grammars and making them easily available for new projects. The first scientific goal is to support grammar engineering for linguistic hypothesis testing, allowing users to quickly customize a basic grammar and use it as a medium in which to develop and test analyses of more interesting phenomena.[3] The second scientific goal is to use computational methods to combine the results of typological research and formal syntactic analysis into a single resource that achieves both typological breadth (handling the known range of realizations of the phenomena analyzed) and analytical depth (producing analyses which work together to map surface strings to semantic representations) (Drellishak, 2009).

2 System Overview

Grammar customization with the LinGO Grammar Matrix consists of three primary activities: filling out the questionnaire, preliminary testing of the grammar fragment, and grammar creation.

2.1 Questionnaire

Most of the linguistic phenomena supported by the questionnaire vary across languages along multiple dimensions. It is not enough, for example,

[1] http://www.delph-in.net/matrix/customize/
[2] http://www.delph-in.net

[3] Research of this type based on the Grammar Matrix includes (Crysmann, 2009) (tone change in Hausa) and (Fokkens et al., 2009) (Turkish suspended affixation).

Proceedings of the ACL 2010 System Demonstrations, pages 1–6,
Uppsala, Sweden, 13 July 2010.

simply to know that the target language has coordination. It is also necessary to know, among other things, what types of phrases can be coordinated, how those phrases are marked, and what patterns of marking appear in the language. Supporting a linguistic phenomenon, therefore, requires eliciting the answers to such questions from the user. The customization system elicits these answers using a detailed, web-based, typological questionnaire, then interprets the answers without human intervention and produces a grammar in the format expected by the LKB (Copestake, 2002), namely TDL (type description language).

The questionnaire is designed for linguists who want to create computational grammars of natural languages, and therefore it freely uses technical linguistic terminology, but avoids, when possible, mentioning the internals of the grammar that will be produced, although a user who intends to extend the grammar will need to become familiar with HPSG and TDL before doing so.

The questionnaire is presented to the user as a series of connected web pages. The first page the user sees (the "main page") contains some introductory text and hyperlinks to direct the user to other sections of the questionnaire ("subpages"). Each subpage contains a set of related questions that (with some exceptions) covers the range of a single Matrix library. The actual questions in the questionnaire are represented by HTML form fields, including: text fields, check boxes, radio buttons, drop-downs, and multi-select drop-downs. The values of these form fields are stored in a "choices file", which is the object passed on to the grammar customization stage.

2.1.1 Unbounded Content

Early versions of the customization system (Bender and Flickinger, 2005; Drellishak and Bender, 2005) only allowed a finite (and small) number of entries for things like lexical types. For instance, users were required to provide exactly one transitive verb type and one intransitive verb type. The current system has an iterator mechanism in the questionnaire that allows for repeated sections, and thus unlimited entries. These repeated sections can also be nested, which allows for much more richly structured information.

The utility of the iterator mechanism is most apparent when filling out the Lexicon subpage. Users can create an arbitrary number of lexical rule "slots", each with an arbitrary number of morphemes which each in turn bear any number of feature constraints. For example, the user could create a tense-agreement morphological slot, which contains multiple portmanteau morphemes each expressing some combination of tense, subject person and subject number values (e.g., French *-ez* expresses 2nd person plural subject agreement together with present tense).

The ability provided by the iterators to create unbounded content facilitates the creation of substantial grammars through the customization system. Furthermore, the system allows users to expand on some iterators while leaving others unspecified, thus modeling complex rule interactions even when it cannot cover features provided by these rules. A user can correctly model the morphotactic framework of the language using "skeletal" lexical rules—those that specify morphemes' forms and their co-occurrence restrictions, but perhaps not their morphosyntactic features. The user can then, post-customization, augment these rules with the missing information.

2.1.2 Dynamic Content

In earlier versions of the customization system, the questionnaire was static. Not only was the number of form fields static, but the questions were the same, regardless of user input. The current questionnaire is more dynamic. When the user loads the customization system's main page or subpages, appropriate HTML is created on the fly on the basis of the information already collected from the user as well as language-independent information provided by the system.

The questionnaire has two kinds of dynamic content: expandable lists for unbounded entry fields, and the population of drop-down selectors. The lists in an iterated section can be expanded or shortened with "Add" and "Delete" buttons near the items in question. Drop-down selectors can be automatically populated in several different ways.[4] These dynamic drop-downs greatly lessen the amount of information the user must remember while filling out the questionnaire and can prevent the user from trying to enter an invalid value. Both of these operations occur without refreshing the page, saving time for the user.

[4]These include: the names of currently-defined features, the currently-defined values of a feature, or the values of variables that match a particular regular expression.

2.2 Validation

It makes no sense to attempt to create a consistent grammar from an empty questionnaire, an incomplete questionnaire, or a questionnaire containing contradictory answers, so the customization system first sends a user's answers through "form validation". This component places a set of arbitrarily complex constraints on the answers provided. The system insists, for example, that the user not state the language contains no determiners but then provide one in the Lexicon subpage. When a question fails form validation, it is marked with a red asterisk in the questionnaire, and if the user hovers the mouse cursor over the asterisk, a pop-up message appears describing how form validation failed. The validation component can also produce warnings (marked with red question marks) in cases where the system can generate a grammar from the user's answers, but we have reason to believe the grammar won't behave as expected. This occurs, for example, when there are no verbal lexical entries provided, yielding a grammar that cannot parse any sentences.

2.3 Creating a Grammar

After the questionnaire has passed validation, the system enables two more buttons on the main page: "Test by Generation" and "Create Grammar". "Test by Generation" allows the user to test the performance of the current state of the grammar without leaving the browser, and is described in §3. "Create Grammar" causes the customization system to output an LKB-compatible grammar that includes all the types in the core Matrix, along with the types from each library, tailored appropriately, according to the specific answers provided for the language described in the questionnaire.

2.4 Summary

This section has briefly presented the structure of the customization system. While we anticipate some future improvements (e.g., visualization tools to assist with designing type hierarchies and morphotactic dependencies), we believe that this system is sufficiently general to support the addition of analyses of many different linguistic phenomena. The system has been used to create starter grammars for more than 40 languages in the context of a graduate grammar engineering course.

To give sense of the size of the grammars produced by the customization system, Table 1 compares the English Resource Grammar (ERG) (Flickinger, 2000), a broad-coverage precision grammar in the same framework under development since 1994, to 11 grammars produced with the customization system by graduate students in a grammar engineering class at the University of Washington. The students developed these grammars over three weeks using reference materials and the customization system. We compare the grammars in terms of the number types they define, as well as the number of lexical rule and phrase structure rule instances.[5] We separate types defined in the Matrix core grammar from language-specific types defined by the customization system. Not all of the Matrix-provided types are used in the definition of the language-specific rules, but they are nonetheless an important part of the grammar, serving as the foundation for further hand-development. The Matrix core grammar includes a larger number of types whose function is to provide disjunctions of parts of speech. These are given in Table 1, as "head types". The final column in the table gives the number of "choices" or specifications that the users gave to the customization system in order to derive these grammars.

3 Test-by-generation

The purpose of the test-by-generation feature is to provide a quick method for testing the grammar compiled from a choices file. It accomplishes this by generating sentences the grammar deems grammatical. This is useful to the user in two main ways: it quickly shows whether any ungrammatical sentences are being licensed by the grammar and, by providing an exhaustive list of licensed sentences for an input template, allows users to see if an expected sentence is not being produced.

It is worth emphasizing that this feature of the customization system relies on the bidirectionality of the grammars; that is, the fact that the same grammar can be used for both parsing and generation. Our experience has shown that grammar developers quickly find generation provides a more stringent test than parsing, especially for the ability of a grammar to model ungrammaticality.

3.1 Underspecified MRS

Testing by generation takes advantage of the generation algorithm include in the LKB (Carroll et al.,

[5]Serious lexicon development is taken as a separate task and thus lexicon size is not included in the table.

Language	Family	Lg-specific types	Matrix types	Head types	Lex rules	Phrasal rules	Choices
ERG	Germanic	3654	N/A	N/A	71	226	N/A
Breton	Celtic	220	413	510	57	49	1692
Cherokee	Iroquoian	182	413	510	95	27	985
French	Romance	137	413	510	29	22	740
Jamamadí	Arauan	188	413	510	87	11	1151
Lushootseed	Salish	95	413	510	20	8	391
Nishnaabemwin	Algonquian	289	413	510	124	50	1754
Pashto	Iranian	234	413	510	86	19	1839
Pali	Indo-Aryan	237	413	510	92	55	1310
Russian	Slavic	190	413	510	56	35	993
Shona	Bantu	136	413	510	51	9	591
Vietnamese	Austro-Asiatic	105	413	510	2	26	362
Average		182.9	413	510	63.5	28.3	1073.5

Table 1: Grammar sizes in comparison to ERG

1999). This algorithm takes input in the form of Minimal Recursion Semantics (MRS) (Copestake et al., 2005): a bag of elementary predications, each bearing features encoding a predicate string, a label, and one or more argument positions that can be filled with variables or with labels of other elementary predications.[6] Each variable can further bear features encoding "variable properties" such as tense, aspect, mood, sentential force, person, number or gender.

In order to test our starter grammars by generation, therefore, we must provide input MRSs. The shared core grammar ensures that all of the grammars produce and interpret valid MRSs, but there are still language-specific properties in these semantic representations. Most notably, the predicate strings are user-defined (and language-specific), as are the variable properties. In addition, some coarser-grained typological properties (such as the presence or absence of determiners) lead to differences in the semantic representations. Therefore, we cannot simply store a set of MRSs from one grammar to use as input to the generator.

Instead, we take a set of stored template MRSs and generalize them by removing all variable properties (allowing the generator to explore all possible values), leaving only the predicate strings and links between the elementary predications. We then replace the stored predicate strings with ones selected from among those provided by the user. Figure 1a shows an MRS produced by a grammar fragment for English. Figure 1b shows the MRS with the variable properties removed and the predicate strings replaced with generic place-holders. One such template is needed for every sentence type (e.g., intransitive, transitive,

a. ⟨ h1,e2, {h7:_cat_n_rel(x4:SG:THIRD),
h3:exist_q_rel(x4, h5, h6),
h1:_sleep_v_rel(e2:PRES, x4)},
{h5 qeq h7} ⟩

b. ⟨ h1,e2, {h7:#NOUN1#(x4),
h3:#DET1#(x4, h5, h6),
h1:#VERB#(e2, x4)},
{h5 qeq h7} ⟩

Figure 1: Original and underspecified MRS

negated-intransitive, etc.). In order to ensure that the generated strings are maximally informative to the user testing a grammar, we take advantage of the lexical type system. Because words in lexical types as defined by the customization system differ only in orthography and predicate string, and not in syntactic behavior, we need only consider one word of each type. This allows us to focus the range of variation produced by the generator on (a) the differences between lexical types and (b) the variable properties.

3.2 Test by generation process

The first step of the test-by-generation process is to compile the choices file into a grammar. Next, a copy of the LKB is initialized on the web server that is hosting the Matrix system, and the newly-created grammar is loaded into this LKB session.

We then construct the underspecified MRSs in order to generate from them. To do this, the process needs to find the proper predicates to use for verbs, nouns, determiners, and any other parts of speech that a given MRS template may require. For nouns and determiners, the choices file is searched for the predicate for one noun of each lexical noun type, all of the determiner predicates, and whether or not each noun type needs a determiner or not. For verbs, the process is more complicated, requiring valence information as well as predicate strings in order to select the correct MRS template. In order to get this information, the process traverses the type hierarchy above the verbal lexical

[6] This latter type of argument encodes scopal dependencies. We abstract away here from the MRS approach to scope underspecification which is nonetheless critical for its computational tractability.

types until it finds a type that gives valence information about the verb. Once the process has all of this information, it matches verbs to MRS templates and fills in appropriate predicates.

The test-by-generation process then sends these constructed MRSs to the LKB process and displays the generation results, along with a brief explanation of the input semantics that gave rise to them, in HTML for the user.[7]

4 Related Work

As stated above, the engineering goal of the Grammar Matrix is to facilitate the rapid development of large-scale precision grammars. The starter grammars output by the customization system are compatible in format and semantic representations with existing DELPH-IN tools, including software for grammar development and for applications including machine translation (Oepen et al., 2007) and robust textual entailment (Bergmair, 2008).

More broadly, the Grammar Matrix is situated in the field of multilingual grammar engineering, or the practice of developing linguistically-motivated grammars for multiple languages within a consistent framework. Other projects in this field include ParGram (Butt et al., 2002; King et al., 2005) (LFG), the CoreGram project[8] (e.g., (Müller, 2009)) (HPSG), and the MetaGrammar project (de la Clergerie, 2005) (TAG).

To our knowledge, however, there is only one other system that elicits typological information about a language and outputs an appropriately customized implemented grammar. The system, described in (Black, 2004) and (Black and Black, 2009), is called PAWS (Parser And Writer for Syntax) and is available for download online.[9] PAWS is being developed by SIL in the context of both descriptive (prose) grammar writing and "computer-assisted related language adaptation", the practice of writing a text in a target language by starting with a translation of that text in a related source language and mapping the words from target to source. Accordingly, the output of PAWS consists of both a prose descriptive grammar and an implemented grammar. The latter is in the format required by PC-PATR (McConnel, 1995), and is used primarily to disambiguate morphological analyses of lexical items in the input string.

Other systems that attempt to elicit linguistic information from a user include the Expedition (McShane and Nirenburg, 2003) and Avenue projects (Monson et al., 2008), which are specifically targeted at developing machine translation for low-density languages. These projects differ from the Grammar Matrix customization system in eliciting information from native speakers (such as paradigms or translations of specifically tailored corpora), rather than linguists. Further, unlike the Grammar Matrix customization system, they do not produce resources meant to sustain further development by a linguist.

5 Demonstration Plan

Our demonstration illustrates how the customization system can be used to create starter grammars and test them by invoking test-by-generation. We first walk through the questionnaire to illustrate the functionality of libraries and the way that the user interacts with the system to enter information. Then, using a sample grammar for English, we demonstrate how test-by-generation can expose both overgeneration (ungrammatical generated strings) and undergeneration (gaps in generated paradigms). Finally, we return to the questionnaire to address the bugs in the sample grammar and retest to show the result.

6 Conclusion

This paper has presented an overview of the LinGO Grammar Matrix Customization System, highlighting the ways in which it provides access to its repository of linguistic knowledge. The current customization system covers a sufficiently wide range of phenomena that the grammars it produces are non-trivial. In addition, it is not always apparent to a user what the implications will be of selecting various options in the questionnaire, nor how analyses of different phenomena will interact. The test-by-generation methodology allows users to interactively explore the consequences of different linguistic analyses within the platform. We anticipate that it will, as a result, encourage users to develop more complex grammars within the customization system (before moving on to hand-editing) and thereby gain more benefit.

[7] This set-up scales well to multiple users, as the user's interaction with the LKB is done once per customized grammar, providing output for the user to peruse as his or her leisure. The LKB process does not persist, but can be started again by reinvoking test-by-generation, such as when the user has updated the grammar definition.

[8] http://hpsg.fu-berlin.de/Projects/core.html

[9] http://www.sil.org/computing/catalog/show_software.asp?id=85

Acknowledgments

This material is based upon work supported by the National Science Foundation under Grant No. 0644097. Any opinions, findings, and conclusions or recommendations expressed in this material are those of the authors and do not necessarily reflect the views of the National Science Foundation.

References

Emily M. Bender and Dan Flickinger. 2005. Rapid prototyping of scalable grammars: Towards modularity in extensions to a language-independent core. In *Proc. of IJCNLP-05 (Posters/Demos)*.

Emily M. Bender, Dan Flickinger, and Stephan Oepen. 2002. The grammar matrix: An open-source starter-kit for the rapid development of cross-linguistically consistent broad-coverage precision grammars. In *Proc. of the Workshop on Grammar Engineering and Evaluation at COLING 2002*, pages 8–14.

Richard Bergmair. 2008. Monte Carlo semantics: McPIET at RTE4. In *Text Analysis Conference (TAC 2008) Workshop-RTE-4 Track. National Institute of Standards and Technology*, pages 17–19.

Cheryl A. Black and H. Andrew Black. 2009. PAWS: Parser and writer for syntax: Drafting syntactic grammars in the third wave. In *SIL Forum for Language Fieldwork*, volume 2.

Cheryl A. Black. 2004. Parser and writer for syntax. Paper presented at the International Conference on Translation with Computer-Assisted Technology: Changes in Research, Teaching, Evaluation, and Practice, University of Rome "La Sapienza", April 2004.

Miriam Butt, Helge Dyvik, Tracy Holloway King, Hiroshi Masuichi, and Christian Rohrer. 2002. The parallel grammar project. In *Proc. of the Workshop on Grammar Engineering and Evaluation at COLING 2002*, pages 1–7.

John Carroll, Ann Copestake, Dan Flickinger, and Victor Poznański. 1999. An efficient chart generator for (semi-) lexicalist grammars. In *Proc. of the 7th European workshop on natural language generation (EWNLG99)*, pages 86–95.

Ann Copestake, Dan Flickinger, Carl Pollard, and Ivan A. Sag. 2005. Minimal recursion semantics: An introduction. *Research on Language & Computation*, 3(4):281–332.

Ann Copestake. 2002. *Implementing Typed Feature Structure Grammars*. CSLI, Stanford.

Berthold Crysmann. 2009. Autosegmental representations in an HPSG for Hausa. In *Proc. of the Workshop on Grammar Engineering Across Frameworks 2009*.

Éric Villemonte de la Clergerie. 2005. From metagrammars to factorized TAG/TIG parsers. In *Proc. of IWPT'05*, pages 190–191.

Scott Drellishak and Emily M. Bender. 2005. A coordination module for a crosslinguistic grammar resource. In Stefan Müller, editor, *Proc. of HPSG 2005*, pages 108–128, Stanford. CSLI.

Scott Drellishak. 2009. *Widespread But Not Universal: Improving the Typological Coverage of the Grammar Matrix*. Ph.D. thesis, University of Washington.

Dan Flickinger. 2000. On building a more efficient grammar by exploiting types. *Natural Language Engineering*, 6:15 – 28.

Antske Fokkens, Laurie Poulson, and Emily M. Bender. 2009. Inflectional morphology in Turkish VP-coordination. In Stefan Müller, editor, *Proc. of HPSG 2009*, pages 110–130, Stanford. CSLI.

Tracy Holloway King, Martin Forst, Jonas Kuhn, and Miriam Butt. 2005. The feature space in parallel grammar writing. *Research on Language & Computation*, 3(2):139–163.

Stephen McConnel. 1995. *PC-PATR Reference Manual*. Summer Institute for Linguistics. http://www.sil.org/pcpatr/manual/pcpatr.html.

Marjorie McShane and Sergei Nirenburg. 2003. Parameterizing and eliciting text elements across languages for use in natural language processing systems. *Machine Translation*, 18:129–165.

Christian Monson, Ariadna Font Llitjs, Vamshi Ambati, Lori Levin, Alon Lavie, Alison Alvarez, Roberto Aranovich, Jaime Carbonell, Robert Frederking, Erik Peterson, and Katharina Probst. 2008. Linguistic structure and bilingual informants help induce machine translation of lesser-resourced languages. In *LREC'08*.

Stefan Müller. 2009. Towards an HPSG analysis of Maltese. In Bernard Comrie, Ray Fabri, Beth Hume, Manwel Mifsud, Thomas Stolz, and Martine Vanhove, editors, *Introducing Maltese linguistics. Papers from the 1st International Conference on Maltese Linguistics*, pages 83–112. Benjamins, Amsterdam.

Stephan Oepen, Erik Velldal, Jan Tore Lnning, Paul Meurer, Victoria Rosn, and Dan Flickinger. 2007. Towards hybrid quality-oriented machine translation. On linguistics and probabilities in MT. In *11th International Conference on Theoretical and Methodological Issues in Machine Translation*.

Carl Pollard and Ivan A. Sag. 1994. *Head-Driven Phrase Structure Grammar*. The University of Chicago Press, Chicago, IL.

cdec: A Decoder, Alignment, and Learning Framework for Finite-State and Context-Free Translation Models

Chris Dyer
University of Maryland
redpony@umd.edu

Adam Lopez
University of Edinburgh
alopez@inf.ed.ac.uk

Juri Ganitkevitch
Johns Hopkins University
juri@cs.jhu.edu

Jonathan Weese
Johns Hopkins University
jweese@cs.jhu.edu

Ferhan Ture
University of Maryland
fture@cs.umd.edu

Phil Blunsom
Oxford University
pblunsom@comlab.ox.ac.uk

Hendra Setiawan
University of Maryland
hendra@umiacs.umd.edu

Vladimir Eidelman
University of Maryland
vlad@umiacs.umd.edu

Philip Resnik
University of Maryland
resnik@umiacs.umd.edu

Abstract

We present `cdec`, an open source framework for decoding, aligning with, and training a number of statistical machine translation models, including word-based models, phrase-based models, and models based on synchronous context-free grammars. Using a single unified internal representation for translation forests, the decoder strictly separates model-specific translation logic from general rescoring, pruning, and inference algorithms. From this unified representation, the decoder can extract not only the 1- or k-best translations, but also alignments to a reference, or the quantities necessary to drive discriminative training using gradient-based or gradient-free optimization techniques. Its efficient C++ implementation means that memory use and runtime performance are significantly better than comparable decoders.

1 Introduction

The dominant models used in machine translation and sequence tagging are formally based on either weighted finite-state transducers (FSTs) or weighted synchronous context-free grammars (SCFGs) (Lopez, 2008). Phrase-based models (Koehn et al., 2003), lexical translation models (Brown et al., 1993), and finite-state conditional random fields (Sha and Pereira, 2003) exemplify the former, and hierarchical phrase-based models the latter (Chiang, 2007). We introduce a software package called `cdec` that manipulates both classes in a unified way.[1]

Although open source decoders for both phrase-based and hierarchical translation models have been available for several years (Koehn et al., 2007; Li et al., 2009), their extensibility to new models and algorithms is limited by two significant design flaws that we have avoided with `cdec`. First, their implementations tightly couple the translation, language model integration (which we call *rescoring*), and pruning algorithms. This makes it difficult to explore alternative translation models without also re-implementing rescoring and pruning logic. In `cdec`, model-specific code is only required to construct a translation forest (§3). *General* rescoring (with language models or other models), pruning, inference, and alignment algorithms then apply to the unified data structure (§4). Hence *all* model types benefit immediately from new algorithms (for rescoring, inference, etc.); new models can be more easily prototyped; and controlled comparison of models is made easier.

Second, existing open source decoders were designed with the traditional phrase-based parameterization using a very small number of dense features (typically less than 10). `cdec` has been designed from the ground up to support any parameterization, from those with a handful of dense features up to models with millions of sparse features (Blunsom et al., 2008; Chiang et al., 2009). Since the inference algorithms necessary to compute a training objective (e.g. conditional likelihood or expected BLEU) and its gradient operate on the unified data structure (§5), any model type can be trained using with any of the supported training

[1] The software is released under the Apache License, version 2.0, and is available from http://cdec-decoder.org/ .

Proceedings of the ACL 2010 System Demonstrations, pages 7–12,
Uppsala, Sweden, 13 July 2010.

criteria. The software package includes general function optimization utilities that can be used for discriminative training (§6).

These features are implemented without compromising on performance. We show experimentally that `cdec` uses less memory and time than comparable decoders on a controlled translation task (§7).

2 Decoder workflow

The decoding pipeline consists of two phases. The first (Figure 1) transforms input, which may be represented as a source language sentence, lattice (Dyer et al., 2008), or context-free forest (Dyer and Resnik, 2010), into a translation forest that has been rescored with all applicable models.

In `cdec`, the only model-specific logic is confined to the first step in the process where an input string (or lattice, etc.) is transduced into the unified hypergraph representation. Since the model-specific code need not worry about integration with rescoring models, it can be made quite simple and efficient. Furthermore, prior to language model integration (and distortion model integration, in the case of phrase based translation), pruning is unnecessary for most kinds of models, further simplifying the model-specific code. Once this unscored translation forest has been generated, any non-coaccessible states (i.e., states that are not reachable from the goal node) are removed and the resulting structure is rescored with language models using a user-specified intersection/pruning strategy (§4) resulting in a rescored translation forest and completing phase 1.

The second phase of the decoding pipeline (depicted in Figure 2) computes a value from the rescored forest: 1- or k-best derivations, feature expectations, or intersection with a target language reference (sentence or lattice). The last option generates an *alignment forest*, from which a word alignment or feature expectations can be extracted. Most of these values are computed in a time complexity that is linear in the number of edges and nodes in the translation hypergraph using `cdec`'s semiring framework (§5).

2.1 Alignment forests and alignment

Alignment is the process of determining if and how a translation model generates a $\langle$*source, target*$\rangle$ string pair. To compute an alignment under a translation model, the phase 1 translation hypergraph is reinterpreted as a synchronous context-free grammar and then used to parse the *target* sentence.[2] This results in an *alignment forest*, which is a compact representation of all the derivations of the sentence pair under the translation model. From this forest, the Viterbi or maximum *a posteriori* word alignment can be generated. This alignment algorithm is explored in depth by Dyer (2010). Note that if the phase 1 forest has been pruned in some way, or the grammar does not derive the sentence pair, the target intersection parse may fail, meaning that an alignment will not be recoverable.

3 Translation hypergraphs

Recent research has proposed a unified representation for the various translation and tagging formalisms that is based on weighted logic programming (Lopez, 2009). In this view, translation (or tagging) deductions have the structure of a *context-free forest*, or directed hypergraph, where edges have a single head and 0 or more tail nodes (Nederhof, 2003). Once a forest has been constructed representing the possible translations, general inference algorithms can be applied.

In `cdec`'s translation hypergraph, a node represents a contiguous sequence of target language words. For SCFG models and sequential tagging models, a node also corresponds to a source span and non-terminal type, but for word-based and phrase-based models, the relationship to the source string (or lattice) may be more complicated. In a phrase-based translation hypergraph, the node will correspond to a source *coverage vector* (Koehn et al., 2003). In word-based models, a single node may derive multiple different source language coverages since word based models impose no requirements on covering all words in the input. Figure 3 illustrates two example hypergraphs, one generated using a SCFG model and other from a phrase-based model.

Edges are associated with exactly one synchronous production in the source and target language, and alternative translation possibilities are expressed as alternative edges. Edges are further annotated with feature values, and are annotated with the source span vector the edge corresponds to. An edge's output label may contain mixtures of terminal symbol yields and positions indicating where a child node's yield should be substituted.

[2]The parser is smart enough to detect the left-branching grammars generated by lexical translation and tagging models, and use a more efficient intersection algorithm.

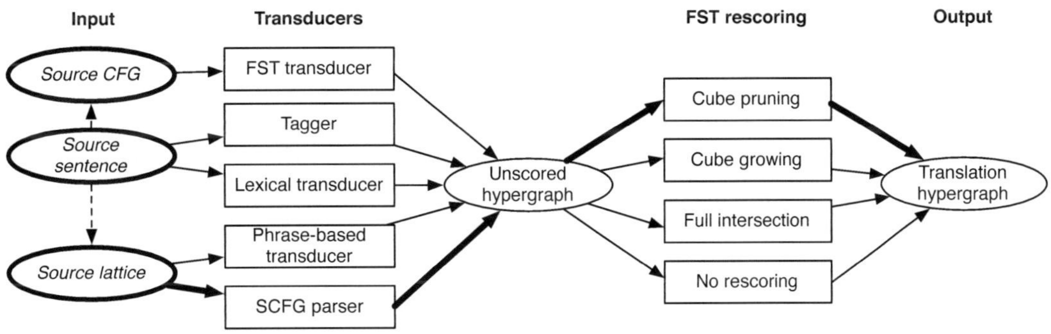

Figure 1: Forest generation workflow (first half of decoding pipeline). The decoder's configuration specifies what path is taken from the input (one of the bold ovals) to a unified translation hypergraph. The highlighted path is the workflow used in the test reported in §7.

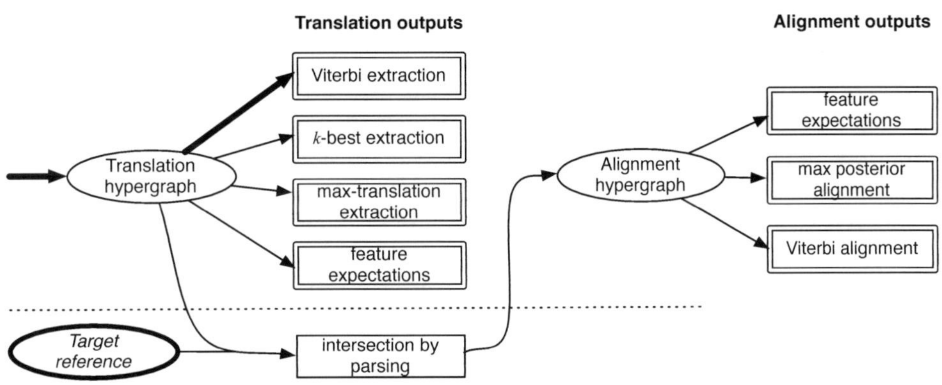

Figure 2: Output generation workflow (second half of decoding pipeline). Possible output types are designated with a double box.

In the case of SCFG grammars, the edges correspond simply to rules in the synchronous grammar. For non-SCFG translation models, there are two kinds of edges. The first have zero tail nodes (i.e., an arity of 0), and correspond to word or phrase translation pairs (with all translation options existing on edges deriving the same head node), or *glue rules* that glue phrases together. For tagging, word-based, and phrase-based models, these are strictly arranged in a monotone, left-branching structure.

4 Rescoring with weighted FSTs

The design of `cdec` separates the creation of a translation forest from its rescoring with a language models or similar models.[3] Since the structure of the unified search space is context free (§3), we use the logic for language model rescoring described by Chiang (2007), although any weighted intersection algorithm can be applied. The rescoring models need not be explicitly represented as FSTs—the state space can be inferred.

Although intersection using the Chiang algorithm runs in polynomial time and space, the resulting rescored forest may still be too large to represent completely. `cdec` therefore supports three pruning strategies that can be used during intersection: full unpruned intersection (useful for tagging models to incorporate, e.g., Markov features, but not generally practical for translation), cube pruning, and cube growing (Huang and Chiang, 2007).

5 Semiring framework

Semirings are a useful mathematical abstraction for dealing with translation forests since many useful quantities can be computed using a single linear-time algorithm but with different semirings. A semiring is a 5-tuple $(\mathbb{K}, \oplus, \otimes, \overline{0}, \overline{1})$ that indicates the set from which the values will be drawn, $\mathbb{K}$, a generic addition and multiplication operation, $\oplus$ and $\otimes$, and their identities $\overline{0}$ and $\overline{1}$. Multiplication and addition must be associative. Multiplication must distribute over addition, and $v \otimes \overline{0}$

[3]Other rescoring models that depend on sequential context include distance-based reordering models or Markov features in tagging models.

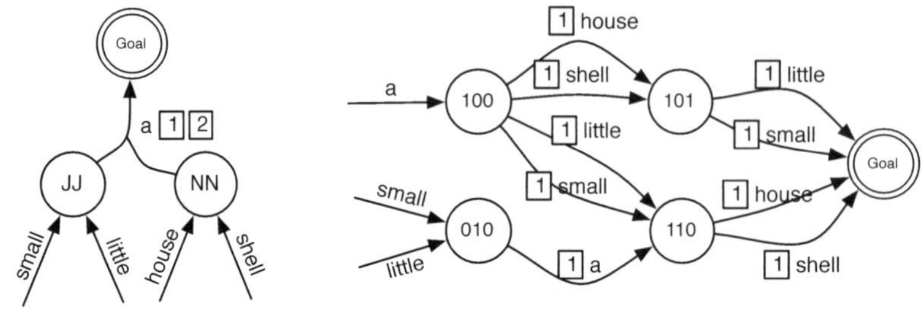

Figure 3: Example unrescored translation hypergraphs generated for the German input *ein* (a) *kleines* (small/little) *Haus* (house/shell) using a SCFG-based model (left) and phrase-based model with a distortion limit of 1 (right).

must equal $\overline{0}$. Values that can be computed using the semirings include the number of derivations, the expected translation length, the entropy of the translation posterior distribution, and the expected values of feature functions (Li and Eisner, 2009).

Since semirings are such a useful abstraction, `cdec` has been designed to facilitate implementation of new semirings. Table 1 shows the C++ representation used for semirings. Note that because of our representation, built-in types like `double`, `int`, and `bool` (together with their default operators) are semirings. Beyond these, the type `prob_t` is provided which stores the logarithm of the value it represents, which helps avoid underflow and overflow problems that may otherwise be encountered. A generic first-order expectation semiring is also provided (Li and Eisner, 2009).

Table 1: Semiring representation. `T` is a C++ type name.

Element	C++ representation
$\mathbb{K}$	`T`
$\oplus$	`T::operator+=`
$\otimes$	`T::operator*=`
$\overline{0}$	`T()`
$\overline{1}$	`T(1)`

Three standard algorithms parameterized with semirings are provided: INSIDE, OUTSIDE, and INSIDEOUTSIDE, and the semiring is specified using C++ generics (templates). Additionally, each algorithm takes a *weight function* that maps from hypergraph edges to a value in $\mathbb{K}$, making it possible to use many different semirings without altering the underlying hypergraph.

5.1 Viterbi and k-best extraction

Although Viterbi and k-best extraction algorithms are often expressed as INSIDE algorithms with the tropical semiring, `cdec` provides a separate derivation extraction framework that makes use of a $<$ operator (Huang and Chiang, 2005). Thus, many of the semiring types define not only the elements shown in Table 1 but `T::operator<` as well. The k-best extraction algorithm is also parameterized by an optional predicate that can filter out derivations at each node, enabling extraction of only derivations that yield different strings as in Huang et al. (2006).

6 Model training

Two training pipelines are provided with `cdec`. The first, called Viterbi envelope semiring training, VEST, implements the minimum error rate training (MERT) algorithm, a gradient-free optimization technique capable of maximizing arbitrary loss functions (Och, 2003).

6.1 VEST

Rather than computing an error surface using k-best approximations of the decoder search space, `cdec`'s implementation performs inference over the full hypergraph structure (Kumar et al., 2009). In particular, by defining a semiring whose values are sets of line segments, having an addition operation equivalent to union, and a multiplication operation equivalent to a linear transformation of the line segments, Och's line search can be computed simply using the INSIDE algorithm. Since the translation hypergraphs generated by `cdec` may be quite large making inference expensive, the logic for constructing error surfaces is factored according to the MapReduce programming paradigm (Dean and Ghemawat, 2004), enabling parallelization across a cluster of machines. Implementations of the BLEU and TER loss functions are provided (Papineni et al., 2002; Snover et al., 2006).

6.2 Large-scale discriminative training

In addition to the widely used MERT algorithm, `cdec` also provides a training pipeline for discriminatively trained probabilistic translation models (Blunsom et al., 2008; Blunsom and Osborne, 2008). In these models, the translation model is trained to maximize conditional log likelihood of the training data under a specified grammar. Since log likelihood is differentiable with respect to the feature weights in an exponential model, it is possible to use gradient-based optimization techniques to train the system, enabling the parameterization of the model using millions of sparse features. While this training approach was originally proposed for SCFG-based translation models, it can be used to train *any* model type in `cdec`. When used with sequential tagging models, this pipeline is identical to traditional sequential CRF training (Sha and Pereira, 2003).

Both the objective (conditional log likelihood) and its gradient have the form of a difference in two quantities: each has one term that is computed over the *translation* hypergraph which is subtracted from the result of the same computation over the *alignment* hypergraph (refer to Figures 1 and 2). The conditional log likelihood is the difference in the log partition of the translation and alignment hypergraph, and is computed using the INSIDE algorithm. The gradient with respect to a particular feature is the difference in this feature's expected value in the translation and alignment hypergraphs, and can be computed using either INSIDEOUTSIDE or the expectation semiring and INSIDE. Since a translation forest is generated as an intermediate step in generating an alignment forest (§2) this computation is straightforward.

Since gradient-based optimization techniques may require thousands of evaluations to converge, the batch training pipeline is split into map and reduce components, facilitating distribution over very large clusters. Briefly, the `cdec` is run as the map function, and sentence pairs are mapped over. The reduce function aggregates the results and performs the optimization using standard algorithms, including LBFGS (Liu et al., 1989), RPROP (Riedmiller and Braun, 1993), and stochastic gradient descent.

7 Experiments

Table 2 compares the performance of `cdec`, Hiero, and Joshua 1.3 (running with 1 or 8 threads) decoding using a hierarchical phrase-based translation grammar and identical pruning settings.[4] Figure 4 shows the `cdec` configuration and weights file used for this test.

The workstation used has two 2GHz quad-core Intel Xenon processors, 32GB RAM, is running Linux kernel version 2.6.18 and gcc version 4.1.2. All decoders use SRI's language model toolkit, version 1.5.9 (Stolcke, 2002). Joshua was run on the Sun HotSpot JVM, version 1.6.0_12. A hierarchical phrase-based translation grammar was extracted for the NIST MT03 Chinese-English translation using a suffix array rule extractor (Lopez, 2007). A non-terminal span limit of 15 was used, and all decoders were configured to use cube pruning with a limit of 30 candidates at each node and no further pruning. All decoders produced a BLEU score between 31.4 and 31.6 (small differences are accounted for by different tie-breaking behavior and OOV handling).

Table 2: Memory usage and average per-sentence running time, in seconds, for decoding a Chinese-English test set.

Decoder	Lang.	Time (s)	Memory
`cdec`	C++	0.37	1.0Gb
Joshua (1×)	Java	0.98	1.5Gb
Joshua (8×)	Java	0.35	2.5Gb
Hiero	Python	4.04	1.1Gb

```
formalism=scfg
grammar=grammar.mt03.scfg.gz
add_pass_through_rules=true
scfg_max_span_limit=15
feature_function=LanguageModel \
    en.3gram.pruned.lm.gz -o 3
feature_function=WordPenalty
intersection_strategy=cube_pruning
cubepruning_pop_limit=30
```

```
LanguageModel 1.12
WordPenalty -4.26
PhraseModel_0 0.963
PhraseModel_1 0.654
PhraseModel_2 0.773
PassThroughRule -20
```

Figure 4: Configuration file (above) and feature weights file (below) used for the decoding test described in §7.

[4] http://sourceforge.net/projects/joshua/

8 Future work

cdec continues to be under active development. We are taking advantage of its modular design to study alternative algorithms for language model integration. Further training pipelines are under development, including minimum risk training using a linearly decomposable approximation of BLEU (Li and Eisner, 2009), and MIRA training (Chiang et al., 2009). All of these will be made publicly available as the projects progress. We are also improving support for parallel training using Hadoop (an open-source implementation of MapReduce).

Acknowledgements

This work was partially supported by the GALE program of the Defense Advanced Research Projects Agency, Contract No. HR0011-06-2-001. Any opinions, findings, conclusions or recommendations expressed in this paper are those of the authors and do not necessarily reflect the views of the sponsors. Further support was provided the EuroMatrix project funded by the European Commission (7th Framework Programme). Discussions with Philipp Koehn, Chris Callison-Burch, Zhifei Li, Lane Schwarz, and Jimmy Lin were likewise crucial to the successful execution of this project.

References

P. Blunsom and M. Osborne. 2008. Probalistic inference for machine translation. In *Proc. of EMNLP*.

P. Blunsom, T. Cohn, and M. Osborne. 2008. A discriminative latent variable model for statistical machine translation. In *Proc. of ACL-HLT*.

P. F. Brown, V. J. Della Pietra, S. A. Della Pietra, and R. L. Mercer. 1993. The mathematics of statistical machine translation: parameter estimation. *Computational Linguistics*, 19(2):263–311.

D. Chiang, K. Knight, and W. Wang. 2009. 11,001 new features for statistical machine translation. In *Proc. of NAACL*, pages 218–226.

D. Chiang. 2007. Hierarchical phrase-based translation. *Comp. Ling.*, 33(2):201–228.

J. Dean and S. Ghemawat. 2004. MapReduce: Simplified data processing on large clusters. In *Proc. of the 6th Symposium on Operating System Design and Implementation (OSDI 2004)*, pages 137–150.

C. Dyer and P. Resnik. 2010. Context-free reordering, finite-state translation. In *Proc. of HLT-NAACL*.

C. Dyer, S. Muresan, and P. Resnik. 2008. Generalizing word lattice translation. In *Proc. of HLT-ACL*.

C. Dyer. 2010. Two monolingual parses are better than one (synchronous parse). In *Proc. of HLT-NAACL*.

L. Huang and D. Chiang. 2005. Better k-best parsing. In *In Proc. of IWPT*, pages 53–64.

L. Huang and D. Chiang. 2007. Forest rescoring: Faster decoding with integrated language models. In *Proc. ACL*.

L. Huang, K. Knight, and A. Joshi. 2006. A syntax-directed translator with extended domain of locality. In *Proc. of AMTA*.

P. Koehn, F. J. Och, and D. Marcu. 2003. Statistical phrase-based translation. In *Proc. of HLT/NAACL*, pages 48–54.

P. Koehn, H. Hoang, A. B. Mayne, C. Callison-Burch, M. Federico, N. Bertoldi, B. Cowan, W. Shen, C. Moran, R. Zens, C. Dyer, O. Bojar, A. Constantin, and E. Herbst. 2007. Moses: Open source toolkit for statistical machine translation. In *Proc. of ACL, Demonstration Session*, pages 177–180, June.

S. Kumar, W. Macherey, C. Dyer, and F. Och. 2009. Efficient minimum error rate training and minimum B ayes-risk decoding for translation hypergraphs and lattices. In *Proc. of ACL*, pages 163–171.

Z. Li and J. Eisner. 2009. First- and second-order expectation semirings with applications to minimum-risk training on translation forests. In *Proc. of EMNLP*, pages 40–51.

Z. Li, C. Callison-Burch, C. Dyer, J. Ganitkevitch, S. Khudanpur, L. Schwartz, W. N. G. Thornton, J. Weese, and O. F. Zaidan. 2009. Joshua: an open source toolkit for parsing-based machine translation. In *Proc. of the Fourth Workshop on Stat. Machine Translation*, pages 135–139.

D. C. Liu, J. Nocedal, D. C. Liu, and J. Nocedal. 1989. On the limited memory BFGS method for large scale optimization. *Mathematical Programming B*, 45(3):503–528.

A. Lopez. 2007. Hierarchical phrase-based translation with suffix arrays. In *Proc. of EMNLP*, pages 976–985.

A. Lopez. 2008. Statistical machine translation. *ACM Computing Surveys*, 40(3), Aug.

A. Lopez. 2009. Translation as weighted deduction. In *Proc. of EACL*, pages 532–540.

M.-J. Nederhof. 2003. Weighted deductive parsing and Knuth's algorithm. *Comp. Ling.*, 29(1):135–143, Mar.

F. Och. 2003. Minimum error rate training in statistical machine translation. In *Proc. of ACL*, pages 160–167.

K. Papineni, S. Roukos, T. Ward, and W.-J. Zhu. 2002. BLEU: a method for automatic evaluation of machine translation. In *Proc. of ACL*, pages 311–318.

M. Riedmiller and H. Braun. 1993. A direct adaptive method for faster backpropagation learning: The RPROP algorithm. In *Proc. of the IEEE international conference on neural networks*, pages 586–591.

F. Sha and F. Pereira. 2003. Shallow parsing with conditional random fields. In *Proc. of NAACL*, pages 134–141.

M. Snover, B. Dorr, R. Schwartz, L. Micciulla, and J. Makhoul. 2006. A study of translation edit rate with targeted human annotation. In *Proc. AMTA*.

A. Stolcke. 2002. SRILM – an extensible language modeling toolkit. In *Intl. Conf. on Spoken Language Processing*.

BEETLE II: a system for tutoring and computational linguistics experimentation

Myroslava O. Dzikovska and **Johanna D. Moore**
School of Informatics, University of Edinburgh, Edinburgh, United Kingdom
{m.dzikovska,j.moore}@ed.ac.uk

Natalie Steinhauser and **Gwendolyn Campbell**
Naval Air Warfare Center Training Systems Division, Orlando, FL, USA
{gwendolyn.campbell,natalie.steihauser}@navy.mil

Elaine Farrow
Heriot-Watt University
Edinburgh, United Kingdom
e.farrow@hw.ac.uk

Charles B. Callaway
University of Haifa
Mount Carmel, Haifa, Israel
ccallawa@gmail.com

Abstract

We present BEETLE II, a tutorial dialogue system designed to accept unrestricted language input and support experimentation with different tutorial planning and dialogue strategies. Our first system evaluation used two different tutorial policies and demonstrated that the system can be successfully used to study the impact of different approaches to tutoring. In the future, the system can also be used to experiment with a variety of natural language interpretation and generation techniques.

1 Introduction

Over the last decade there has been a lot of interest in developing tutorial dialogue systems that understand student explanations (Jordan et al., 2006; Graesser et al., 1999; Aleven et al., 2001; Buckley and Wolska, 2007; Nielsen et al., 2008; VanLehn et al., 2007), because high percentages of self-explanation and student contentful talk are known to be correlated with better learning in human-human tutoring (Chi et al., 1994; Litman et al., 2009; Purandare and Litman, 2008; Steinhauser et al., 2007). However, most existing systems use pre-authored tutor responses for addressing student errors. The advantage of this approach is that tutors can devise remediation dialogues that are highly tailored to specific misconceptions many students share, providing step-by-step scaffolding and potentially suggesting additional problems. The disadvantage is a lack of adaptivity and generality: students often get the same remediation for the same error regardless of their past performance or dialogue context, as it is infeasible to author a different remediation dialogue for every possible dialogue state. It also becomes more difficult to experiment with different tutorial policies within the system due to the inherent completixites in applying tutoring strategies consistently across a large number of individual hand-authored remediations.

The BEETLE II system architecture is designed to overcome these limitations (Callaway et al., 2007). It uses a deep parser and generator, together with a domain reasoner and a diagnoser, to produce detailed analyses of student utterances and generate feedback automatically. This allows the system to consistently apply the same tutorial policy across a range of questions. To some extent, this comes at the expense of being able to address individual student misconceptions. However, the system's modular setup and extensibility make it a suitable testbed for both computational linguistics algorithms and more general questions about theories of learning.

A distinguishing feature of the system is that it is based on an introductory electricity and electronics course developed by experienced instructional designers. The course was first created for use in a human-human tutoring study, without taking into account possible limitations of computer tutoring. The exercises were then transferred into a computer system with only minor adjustments (e.g., breaking down compound questions into individual questions). This resulted in a realistic tutoring setup, which presents interesting challenges to language processing components, involving a wide variety of language phenomena.

We demonstrate a version of the system that has undergone a successful user evaluation in

Proceedings of the ACL 2010 System Demonstrations, pages 13–18,
Uppsala, Sweden, 13 July 2010.

2009. The evaluation results indicate that additional improvements to remediation strategies, and especially to strategies dealing with interpretation problems, are necessary for effective tutoring. At the same time, the successful large-scale evaluation shows that BEETLE II can be used as a platform for future experimentation.

The rest of this paper discusses the BEETLE II system architecture (Section 2), system evaluation (Section 3), and the range of computational linguistics problems that can be investigated using BEETLE II (Section 4).

2 System Architecture

The BEETLE II system delivers basic electricity and electronics tutoring to students with no prior knowledge of the subject. A screenshot of the system is shown in Figure 1. The student interface includes an area to display reading material, a circuit simulator, and a dialogue history window. All interactions with the system are typed. Students read pre-authored curriculum slides and carry out exercises which involve experimenting with the circuit simulator and explaining the observed behavior. The system also asks some high-level questions, such as "What is voltage?".

The system architecture is shown in Figure 2. The system uses a standard interpretation pipeline, with domain-independent parsing and generation components supported by domain specific reasoners for decision making. The architecture is discussed in detail in the rest of this section.

2.1 Interpretation Components

We use the TRIPS dialogue parser (Allen et al., 2007) to parse the utterances. The parser provides a domain-independent semantic representation including high-level word senses and semantic role labels. The contextual interpreter then uses a reference resolution approach similar to Byron (2002), and an ontology mapping mechanism (Dzikovska et al., 2008a) to produce a domain-specific semantic representation of the student's output. Utterance content is represented as a set of extracted objects and relations between them. Negation is supported, together with a heuristic scoping algorithm. The interpreter also performs basic ellipsis resolution. For example, it can determine that in the answer to the question "Which bulbs will be on and which bulbs will be off in this diagram?", "off" can be taken to mean "all bulbs in the diagram will be off." The resulting output is then passed on to the domain reasoning and diagnosis components.

2.2 Domain Reasoning and Diagnosis

The system uses a knowledge base implemented in the KM representation language (Clark and Porter, 1999; Dzikovska et al., 2006) to represent the state of the world. At present, the knowledge base represents 14 object types and supports the curriculum containing over 200 questions and 40 different circuits.

Student explanations are checked on two levels, verifying *factual* and *explanation* correctness. For example, for a question "Why is bulb A lit?", if the student says "it is in a closed path", the system checks two things: a) is the bulb indeed in a closed path? and b) is being in a closed path a reasonable explanation for the bulb being lit? Different remediation strategies need to be used depending on whether the student made a factual error (i.e., they misread the diagram and the bulb is not in a closed path) or produced an incorrect explanation (i.e., the bulb is indeed in a closed path, but they failed to mention that a battery needs to be in the same closed path for the bulb to light).

The knowledge base is used to check the factual correctness of the answers first, and then a diagnoser checks the explanation correctness. The diagnoser, based on Dzikovska et al. (2008b), outputs a diagnosis which consists of lists of correct, contradictory and non-mentioned objects and relations from the student's answer. At present, the system uses a heuristic matching algorithm to classify relations into the appropriate category, though in the future we may consider a classifier similar to Nielsen et al. (2008).

2.3 Tutorial Planner

The tutorial planner implements a set of generic tutoring strategies, as well as a policy to choose an appropriate strategy at each point of the interaction. It is designed so that different policies can be defined for the system. The currently implemented strategies are: acknowledging the correct part of the answer; suggesting a slide to read with background material; prompting for missing parts of the answer; hinting (low- and high- specificity); and giving away the answer. Two or more strategies can be used together if necessary.

The hint selection mechanism generates hints automatically. For a low specificity hint it selects

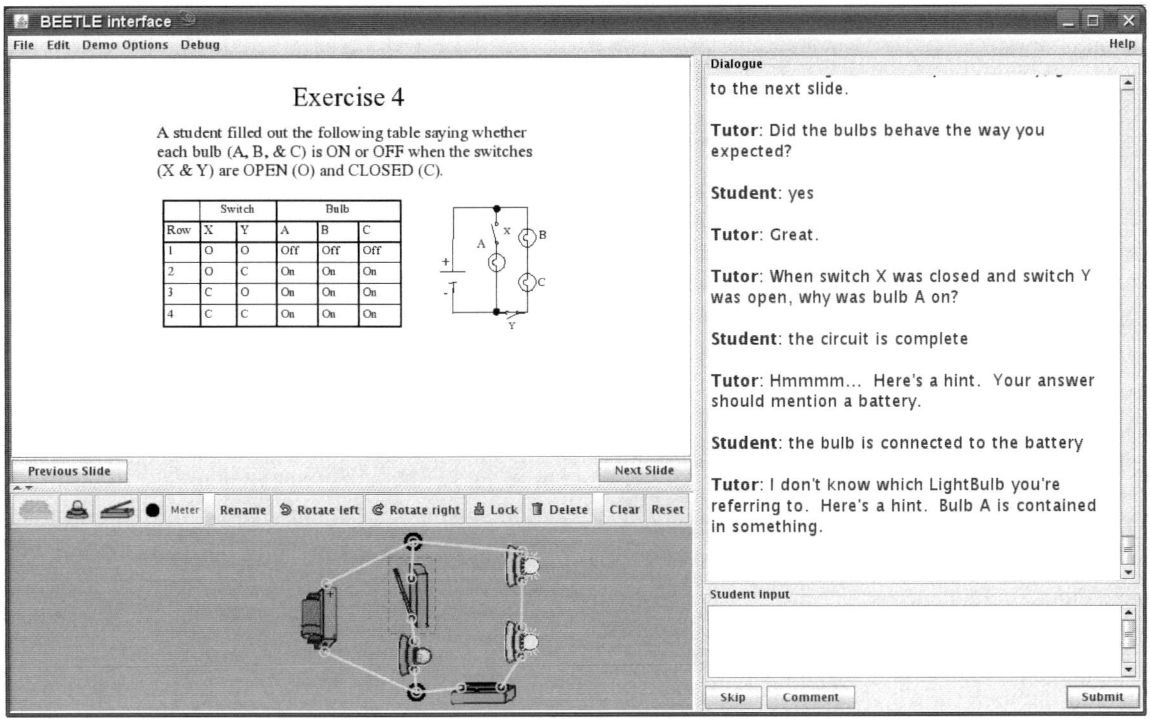

Figure 1: Screenshot of the BEETLE II system

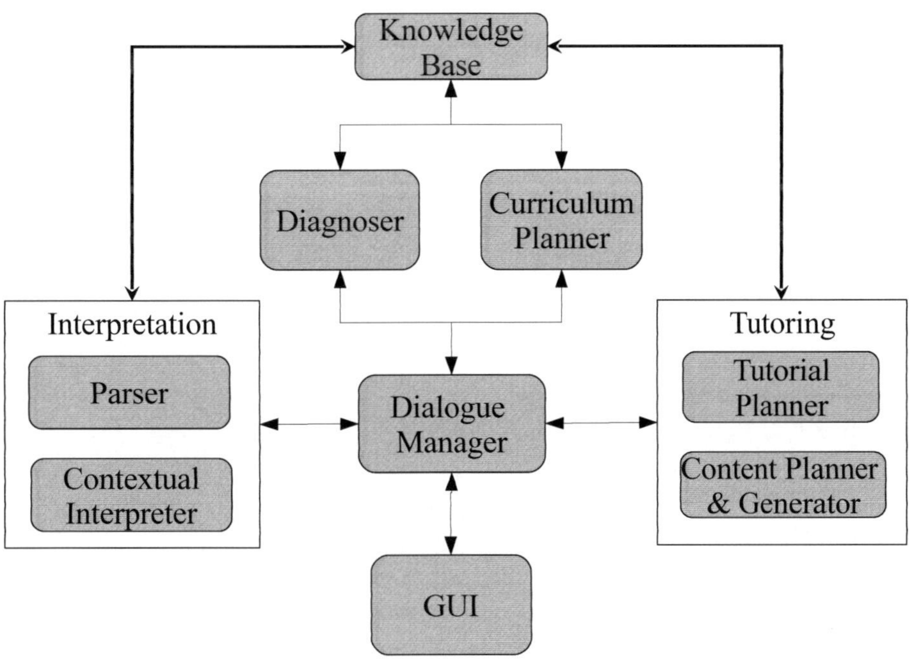

Figure 2: System architecture diagram

an as-yet unmentioned object and hints at it, for example, "Here's a hint: Your answer should mention a battery." For high-specificity, it attempts to hint at a two-place relation, for example, "Here's a hint: the battery is connected to something."

The tutorial policy makes a high-level decision as to which strategy to use (for example, "acknowledge the correct part and give a high specificity hint") based on the answer analysis and dialogue context. At present, the system takes into consideration the number of incorrect answers received in response to the current question and the number of uninterpretable answers.[1]

In addition to a remediation policy, the tutorial planner implements an error recovery policy (Dzikovska et al., 2009). Since the system accepts unrestricted input, interpretation errors are unavoidable. Our recovery policy is modeled on the TargetedHelp (Hockey et al., 2003) policy used in task-oriented dialogue. If the system cannot find an interpretation for an utterance, it attempts to produce a message that describes the problem but without giving away the answer, for example, "I'm sorry, I'm having a problem understanding. I don't know the word *power*." The help message is accompanied with a hint at the appropriate level, also depending on the number of previous incorrect and non-interpretable answers.

2.4 Generation

The strategy decision made by the tutorial planner, together with relevant semantic content from the student's answer (e.g., part of the answer to confirm), is passed to content planning and generation. The system uses a domain-specific content planner to produce input to the surface realizer based on the strategy decision, and a FUF/SURGE (Elhadad and Robin, 1992) generation system to produce the appropriate text. Templates are used to generate some stock phrases such as "When you are ready, go on to the next slide."

2.5 Dialogue Management

Interaction between components is coordinated by the dialogue manager which uses the information-state approach (Larsson and Traum, 2000). The dialogue state is represented by a cumulative answer analysis which tracks, over multiple turns, the correct, incorrect, and not-yet-mentioned parts of the answer. Once the complete answer has been accumulated, the system accepts it and moves on. Tutor hints can contribute parts of the answer to the cumulative state as well, allowing the system to jointly construct the solution with the student.

3 Evaluation

The first experimental evaluation involving 81 participants (undergraduates recruited from a Southeastern University in the USA) was completed in 2009. Participants had little or no prior knowledge of the domain. Each participant took a pre-test, worked through a lesson with the system, took a post-test, and completed a user satisfaction survey. Each session lasted approximately 4 hours.

We implemented two different tutoring policies in the system for this evaluation. The baseline policy used an "accept and bottom out" strategy for all student answers, regardless of their content. The students were always given the correct answer, but the system made no attempt at remediation, and never indicated whether the student was understood (or correct). In comparison, the full adaptive policy attempted to select an appropriate strategy based on student answer analysis and dialogue context, as described above. Students were randomly assigned to a condition. On average, each student session contained 232 student language turns in the fully adaptive condition ($SD = 25.6$) and 156 turns in the baseline condition ($SD = 2.02$). Additional time was taken by reading and interacting with the simulation environment.

Out of 81 students, 76 successfully completed the evaluation (data from 5 participants had to be discarded due to system crashes). There was no significant difference in learning gain between the two conditions (baseline: $M = 0.63, SD = 0.26$, full: $M = 0.57, SD = 0.23$, t-test $p = 0.32$), and students gave higher satisfaction scores to the baseline condition (baseline: $M = 3.32, SD = 0.65$, full: $M = 2.56, SD = 0.65$, t-test, $p < 0.01$). We are currently analyzing the data to investigate the reasons for this outcome. However, the evaluation demonstrated that the system can be successfully deployed in experiments with naive users and therefore can be used to study the impact of different natural language processing algorithms on learning gain and user satisfaction.

An example dialogue with the system, taken from the evaluation corpus, is shown in Figure 3.

[1] Other factors such as student confidence could be considered as well (Callaway et al., 2007).

Tutor:	Why was bulb A on when switch Y was open and switch Z was closed?
Student:	because it had a closed path
Tutor:	Right. There is a closed path. Keep going.
Student:	there was a closed path not effected by the switch
Tutor:	I'm sorry, I'm having a problem understanding. I don't understand the word 'effect' here. Here's a hint. Your answer should mention a battery.
Student:	it has a closed path with the battery
Tutor:	You're on the right track. Here's the answer. Bulb A is still contained in a closed path with the battery.

Figure 3: Example interaction with the system from our corpus

It shows three key system properties: after the student's first turn, the system rephrases its understanding of the correct part of the student answer and prompts the student to supply the missing information. In the second turn, the student utterance could not be interpreted and the system responds with a targeted help message and a hint about the object that needs to be mentioned. Finally, in the last turn the system combines the information from the tutor's hint and the student's answers and restates the complete answer since the current answer was completed over multiple turns.

4 Conclusions and Future Work

The BEETLE II system we present was built to serve as a platform for research in computational linguistics and tutoring, and can be used for task-based evaluation of algorithms developed for other domains. We are currently developing an annotation scheme for the data we collected to identify student paraphrases of correct answers. The annotated data will be used to evaluate the accuracy of existing paraphrasing and textual entailment approaches and to investigate how to combine such algorithms with the current deep linguistic analysis to improve system robustness. We also plan to annotate the data we collected for evidence of misunderstandings, i.e., situations where the system arrived at an incorrect interpretation of a student utterance and took action on it. Such annotation can provide useful input for statistical learning algorithms to detect and recover from misunderstandings.

In dialogue management and generation, the key issue we are planning to investigate is that of linguistic alignment. The analysis of the data we have collected indicates that student satisfaction may be affected if the system rephrases student answers using different words (for example, using better terminology) but doesn't explicitly explain the reason why different terminology is needed (Dzikovska et al., 2010). Results from other systems show that measures of semantic coherence between a student and a system were positively associated with higher learning gain (Ward and Litman, 2006). Using a deep generator to automatically generate system feedback gives us a level of control over the output and will allow us to devise experiments to study those issues in more detail.

From the point of view of tutoring research, we are planning to use the system to answer questions about the effectiveness of different approaches to tutoring, and the differences between human-human and human-computer tutoring. Previous comparisons of human-human and human-computer dialogue were limited to systems that asked short-answer questions (Litman et al., 2006; Rosé and Torrey, 2005). Having a system that allows more unrestricted language input will provide a more balanced comparison. We are also planning experiments that will allow us to evaluate the effectiveness of individual strategies implemented in the system by comparing system versions using different tutoring policies.

Acknowledgments

This work has been supported in part by US Office of Naval Research grants N000140810043 and N0001410WX20278. We thank Katherine Harrison and Leanne Taylor for their help running the evaluation.

References

V. Aleven, O. Popescu, and K. R. Koedinger. 2001. Towards tutorial dialog to support self-explanation: Adding natural language understanding to a cognitive tutor. In *Proceedings of the 10th International Conference on Artificial Intelligence in Education (AIED '01)"*.

James Allen, Myroslava Dzikovska, Mehdi Manshadi, and Mary Swift. 2007. Deep linguistic processing for spoken dialogue systems. In *Proceedings of the ACL-07 Workshop on Deep Linguistic Processing*.

Mark Buckley and Magdalena Wolska. 2007. Towards modelling and using common ground in tutorial dialogue. In *Proceedings of DECALOG, the 2007 Workshop on the Semantics and Pragmatics of Dialogue*, pages 41–48.

Donna K. Byron. 2002. *Resolving Pronominal Reference to Abstract Entities*. Ph.D. thesis, University of Rochester.

Charles B. Callaway, Myroslava Dzikovska, Elaine Farrow, Manuel Marques-Pita, Colin Matheson, and Johanna D. Moore. 2007. The Beetle and BeeDiff tutoring systems. In *Proceedings of SLaTE'07 (Speech and Language Technology in Education)*.

Michelene T. H. Chi, Nicholas de Leeuw, Mei-Hung Chiu, and Christian LaVancher. 1994. Eliciting self-explanations improves understanding. *Cognitive Science*, 18(3):439–477.

Peter Clark and Bruce Porter, 1999. *KM (1.4): Users Manual*. http://www.cs.utexas.edu/users/mfkb/km.

Myroslava O. Dzikovska, Charles B. Callaway, and Elaine Farrow. 2006. Interpretation and generation in a knowledge-based tutorial system. In *Proceedings of EACL-06 workshop on knowledge and reasoning for language processing*, Trento, Italy, April.

Myroslava O. Dzikovska, James F. Allen, and Mary D. Swift. 2008a. Linking semantic and knowledge representations in a multi-domain dialogue system. *Journal of Logic and Computation*, 18(3):405–430.

Myroslava O. Dzikovska, Gwendolyn E. Campbell, Charles B. Callaway, Natalie B. Steinhauser, Elaine Farrow, Johanna D. Moore, Leslie A. Butler, and Colin Matheson. 2008b. Diagnosing natural language answers to support adaptive tutoring. In *Proceedings 21st International FLAIRS Conference*, Coconut Grove, Florida, May.

Myroslava O. Dzikovska, Charles B. Callaway, Elaine Farrow, Johanna D. Moore, Natalie B. Steinhauser, and Gwendolyn C. Campbell. 2009. Dealing with interpretation errors in tutorial dialogue. In *Proceedings of SIGDIAL-09*, London, UK, Sep.

Myroslava O. Dzikovska, Johanna D. Moore, Natalie Steinhauser, and Gwendolyn Campbell. 2010. The impact of interpretation problems on tutorial dialogue. In *Proceedings of the 48th Annual Meeting of the Association for Computational Linguistics(ACL-2010)*.

Michael Elhadad and Jacques Robin. 1992. Controlling content realization with functional unification grammars. In R. Dale, E. Hovy, D. Rösner, and O. Stock, editors, *Proceedings of the Sixth International Workshop on Natural Language Generation*, pages 89–104, Berlin, April. Springer-Verlag.

A. C. Graesser, P. Wiemer-Hastings, P. Wiemer-Hastings, and R. Kreuz. 1999. Autotutor: A simulation of a human tutor. *Cognitive Systems Research*, 1:35–51.

Beth Ann Hockey, Oliver Lemon, Ellen Campana, Laura Hiatt, Gregory Aist, James Hieronymus, Alexander Gruenstein, and John Dowding. 2003. Targeted help for spoken dialogue systems: intelligent feedback improves naive users' performance. In *Proceedings of the tenth conference on European chapter of the Association for Computational Linguistics*, pages 147–154, Morristown, NJ, USA.

Pamela Jordan, Maxim Makatchev, Umarani Pappuswamy, Kurt VanLehn, and Patricia Albacete. 2006. A natural language tutorial dialogue system for physics. In *Proceedings of the 19th International FLAIRS conference*.

Staffan Larsson and David Traum. 2000. Information state and dialogue management in the TRINDI Dialogue Move Engine Toolkit. *Natural Language Engineering*, 6(3-4):323–340.

Diane Litman, Carolyn P. Rosé, Kate Forbes-Riley, Kurt VanLehn, Dumisizwe Bhembe, and Scott Silliman. 2006. Spoken versus typed human and computer dialogue tutoring. *International Journal of Artificial Intelligence in Education*, 16:145–170.

Diane Litman, Johanna Moore, Myroslava Dzikovska, and Elaine Farrow. 2009. Generalizing tutorial dialogue results. In *Proceedings of 14th International Conference on Artificial Intelligence in Education (AIED)*, Brighton, UK, July.

Rodney D. Nielsen, Wayne Ward, and James H. Martin. 2008. Learning to assess low-level conceptual understanding. In *Proceedings 21st International FLAIRS Conference*, Coconut Grove, Florida, May.

Amruta Purandare and Diane Litman. 2008. Content-learning correlations in spoken tutoring dialogs at word, turn and discourse levels. In *Proceedings 21st International FLAIRS Conference*, Coconut Grove, Florida, May.

C.P. Rosé and C. Torrey. 2005. Interactivity versus expectation: Eliciting learning oriented behavior with tutorial dialogue systems. In *Proceedings of Interact'05*.

N. B. Steinhauser, L. A. Butler, and G. E. Campbell. 2007. Simulated tutors in immersive learning environments: Empirically-derived design principles. In *Proceedings of the 2007 Interservice/Industry Training, Simulation and Education Conference*, Orlando, FL.

Kurt VanLehn, Pamela Jordan, and Diane Litman. 2007. Developing pedagogically effective tutorial dialogue tactics: Experiments and a testbed. In *Proceedings of SLaTE Workshop on Speech and Language Technology in Education*, Farmington, PA, October.

Arthur Ward and Diane Litman. 2006. Cohesion and learning in a tutorial spoken dialog system. In *Proceedings of 19th International FLAIRS (Florida Artificial Intelligence Research Society) Conference*, Melbourne Beach, FL.

GernEdiT: A Graphical Tool for GermaNet Development

Verena Henrich
University of Tübingen
Tübingen, Germany.
verena.henrich@uni-tuebingen.de

Erhard Hinrichs
University of Tübingen
Tübingen, Germany.
erhard.hinrichs@uni-tuebingen.de

Abstract

GernEdiT (short for: GermaNet Editing Tool) offers a graphical interface for the lexicographers and developers of GermaNet to access and modify the underlying GermaNet resource. GermaNet is a lexical-semantic wordnet that is modeled after the Princeton WordNet for English. The traditional lexicographic development of GermaNet was error prone and time-consuming, mainly due to a complex underlying data format and no opportunity of automatic consistency checks. GernEdiT replaces the earlier development by a more user-friendly tool, which facilitates automatic checking of internal consistency and correctness of the linguistic resource. This paper presents all these core functionalities of GernEdiT along with details about its usage and usability.

1 Introduction

The main purpose of the GermaNet Editing Tool GernEdiT tool is to support lexicographers in accessing, modifying, and extending the GermaNet data (Kunze and Lemnitzer, 2002; Henrich and Hinrichs, 2010) in an easy and adaptive way and to aid in the navigation through the GermaNet word class hierarchies, so as to find the appropriate place in the hierarchy for new synsets (short for: synonymy set) and lexical units. GernEdiT replaces the traditional GermaNet development based on lexicographer files (Fellbaum, 1998) by a more user-friendly visual tool that supports versioning and collaborative annotation by several lexicographers working in parallel.

Furthermore, GernEdiT facilitates internal consistency of the GermaNet data such as appropriate linking of lexical units with synsets, connectedness of the synset graph, and automatic closure among relations and their inverse counterparts.

All these functionalities along with the main aspects of GernEdiT's usage and usability are presented in this paper.

2 The Structure of GermaNet

GermaNet is a lexical-semantic wordnet that is modeled after the Princeton WordNet for English (Fellbaum, 1998). It covers the three word categories of adjectives, nouns, and verbs and partitions the lexical space into a set of concepts that are interlinked by semantic relations. A semantic concept is modeled by a *synset*. A synset is a set of words (called *lexical units*) where all the words are taken to have (almost) the same meaning. Thus a synset is a set-representation of the semantic relation of synonymy, which means that it consists of a list of lexical units.

There are two types of semantic relations in GermaNet: *conceptual* and *lexical relations*. Conceptual relations hold between two semantic concepts, i.e. synsets. They include relations such as hyperonymy, part-whole relations, entailment, or causation. GermaNet is hierarchically structured in terms of the hyperonymy relation. Lexical relations hold between two individual lexical units. Antonymy, a pair of opposites, is an example of a lexical relation.

3 The GermaNet Editing Tool

The GermaNet Editing Tool GernEdiT provides a graphical user interface, implemented as a Java Swing application, which primarily allows maintaining the GermaNet data in a user-friendly way. The editor represents an interface to a relational database, where all GermaNet data is stored from now on.

Proceedings of the ACL 2010 System Demonstrations, pages 19–24,
Uppsala, Sweden, 13 July 2010.

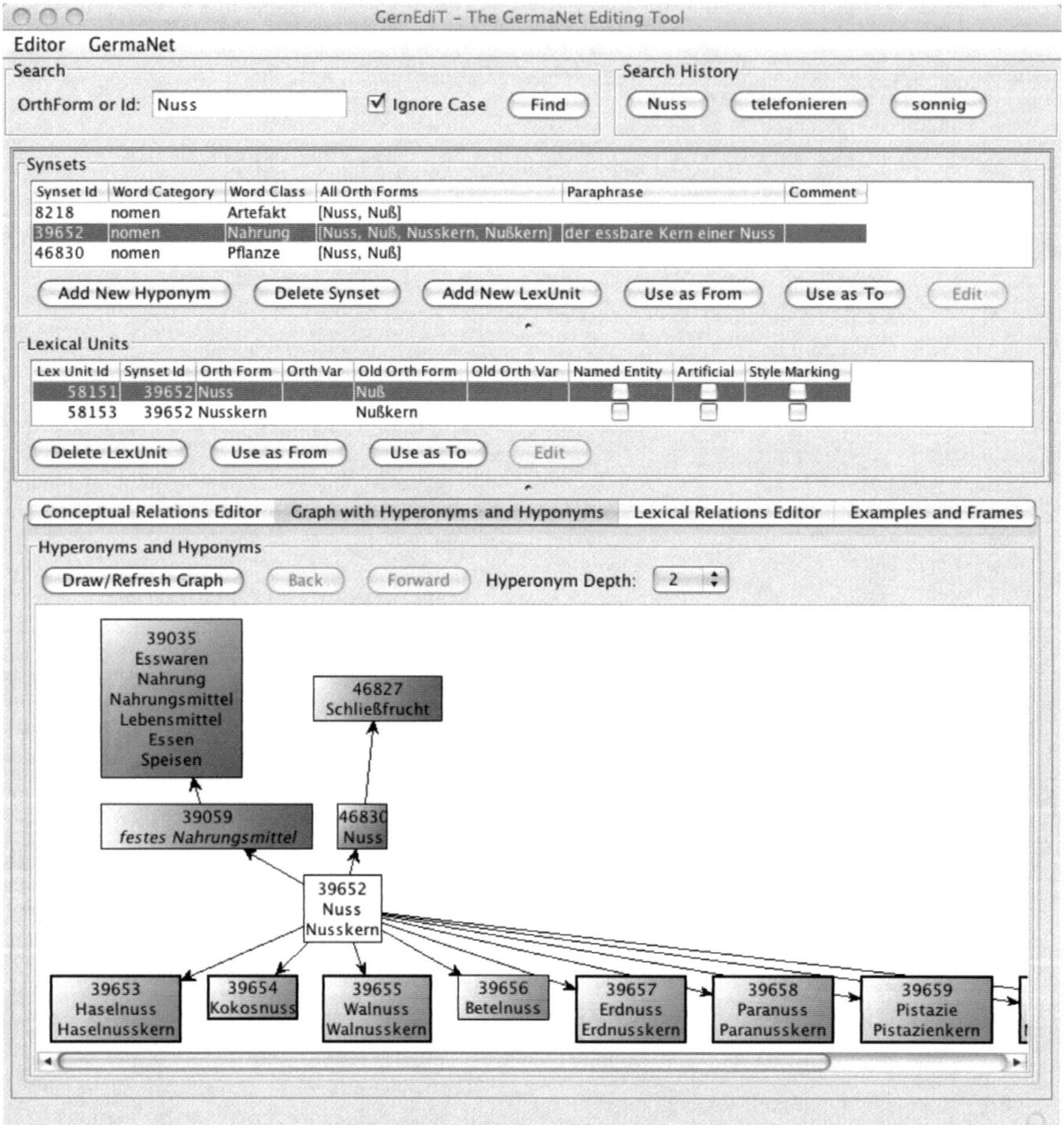

Figure 1. The main view of GernEdiT.

3.1 Motivation

The traditional lexicographic development of GermaNet was error prone and time-consuming, mainly due to a complex underlying data format and no opportunity of automatic consistency checks. This is exactly why GernEdiT was developed: It supports lexicographers who need to access, modify, and extend GermaNet data by providing these functions through simple button-clicks, searches, and form editing. There are several ways to search data and browse through the GermaNet graph. These functionalities allow lexicographers, among other things, to find the appropriate place in the hierarchy for the insertion of new synsets and lexical units. Last but not least, GernEdiT facilitates internal consistency and correctness of the linguistic resource and supports versioning and collaborative annotation of GermaNet by several lexicographers working in parallel.

3.2 The Main User Interface

Figure 1 illustrates the main user panel of GernEdiT. It shows a *Search* panel above, two panels for *Synsets* and *Lexical Units* in the middle, and four tabs below: a *Conceptual Relations Editor*, a *Graph with Hyperonyms and Hyponyms*, a *Lexi-*

Figure 2: Filtered list of lexical units.

cal Relations Editor, and an *Examples and Frames* tab.

In Figure 1, a search for synsets consisting of lexical units with the word *Nuss* (German noun for: *nut*) has been executed. Accordingly, the *Synsets* panel displays the three resulting synsets that match the search item. The *Synset Id* is the unique database ID that unambiguously identifies a synset, and which can also be used to search for exactly that synset. *Word Category* specifies whether a synset is an adjective (*adj*), a noun (*nomen*), or a verb (*verben*), whereas *Word Class* classifies the synsets into semantic fields. The word class of the selected synset in Figure 1 is *Nahrung* (German noun for: *food*). The *Paraphrase* column contains a description of a synset, e.g., for the selected synset the paraphrase is: *der essbare Kern einer Nuss* (German phrase for: *the edible kernel of a nut*). The column *All Orth Forms* simply lists all orthographical variants of all its lexical units.

Which lexical units are listed in the *Lexical Units* panel depends on the selected synset in the *Synsets* panel. Here, *Lex Unit Id* and *Synset Id* again reflect the corresponding unique database IDs. *Orth Form* (short for: *orthographic form*) represents the correct spelling of a word according to the rules of the spelling reform *Neue Deutsche Rechtschreibung* (Rat für deutsche Rechtschreibung, 2006), a recently adopted spelling reform. In our example, the main orthographic form is *Nuss*. *Orth Var* may contain an alternative spelling that is admissible according to the *Neue Deutsche Rechtschreibung.*[1] *Old Orth Form* represents the main orthographic form prior to the *Neue Deutsche Rechtschreibung*. This means that *Nuß* was the correct spelling instead of *Nuss* before the German spelling reform. *Old Orth Var* contains any accepted variant prior to the *Neue Deutsche Rechtschreibung*. The *Old Orth Var* field is filled only if it is no longer allowed in the new orthography.

The Boolean values *Named Entity*, *Artificial*, and *Style Marking* express further properties of a lexical unit, whether the lexical unit is a named entity, an artificial concept node, or a stylistic variant.

For both the lexical units and the synsets, there are two buttons *Use as From* and *Use as To*, which help to add new relations (see the explanation of Figure 3 in section 3.6 below which explains the creation of new relations).

3.3 Search Functionalities

It is possible to search for words or synset database IDs via the search panel (see Figure 1 at the top). The check box *Ignore Case* offers the possibility of searching without distinguishing between upper and lower case.

[1] An example of this kind is the German word *Delfin* (German noun for: *dolphin*). Apart from the main form *Delfin*, there is an orthographic variant *Delphin*.

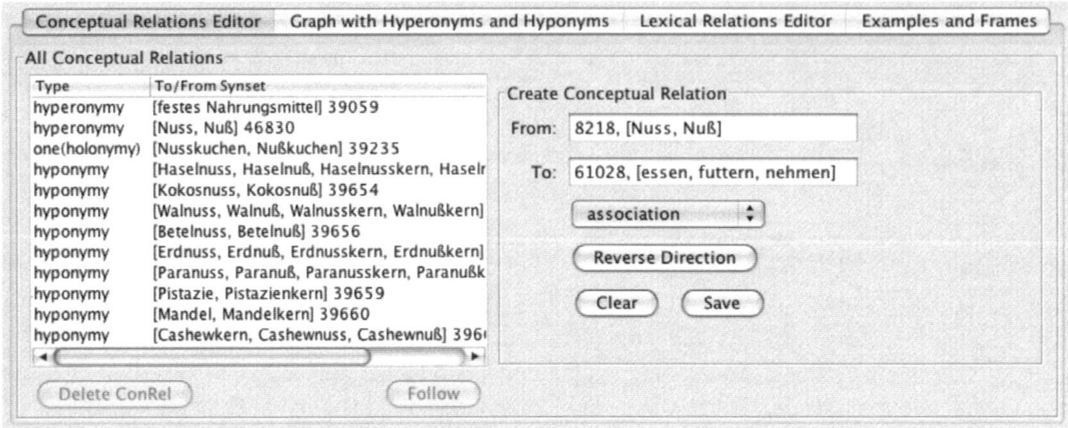

Figure 3. Conceptual Relations Editor tab.

Via the file menu, lists of all synsets or lexical units with their properties can be accessed. To these lists, very detailed filters can be applied: e.g., filtering the lexical units or synsets by parts of their orthographical forms. Figure 2 shows a list of lexical units to which a detailed filter has been applied: verbs have been chosen (see the chosen tab) whose orthographical forms start with an *a-* (see *starts with* check box and corresponding text field) and end with the suffix *-ten* (see *ends with* check box and corresponding text field). Only verbs that have a frame that contains *NN* are chosen (see *Frame contains* check box and corresponding text field). Furthermore, the resulting filtered list is sorted in descending order by their examples (see the little triangle in the *Examples* header of the result table). The number in the brackets behind the word category in the tab title indicates the count of the filtered lexical units (in this example 193 verbs pass the filter).

3.4 Visualization of the Graph Hierarchy

There is the possibility to display a graph with all hyperonyms and hyponyms of a selected synset. This is shown in the bottom half of Figure 1 in the tab *Graph with Hyperonyms and Hyponyms*. The graph in Figure 1 visualizes a part of the hierarchical structure of GermaNet centered around the synset containing *Nuss* and displays the hyperonyms and hyponyms of this synset up to a certain parameterized depth (in this case depth 2 has been chosen). The *Hyperonym Depth* chooser allows unfolding the graph to the top up to the preselected depth. As it is not possible to visualize the whole GermaNet contents at once, the graph can be seen as a window to GermaNet. A click on any synset node within the graph, navigates to that synset. This functionality supports lexicographers especially in finding the appropriate place in the hierarchy for the insertion of new synsets.

3.5 Modifications of Existing Items

If the lexicographers' task is to modify existing synsets or lexical units, this is done by selecting a synset or lexical unit displayed in the *Synsets* and the *Lexical Units* panels shown in Figure 1. The properties of such selected items can be edited by a click in the corresponding table cell. For example by clicking in the cell *Orth Form* the spelling of a lexical unit can be corrected in case of an earlier typo was made.

If lexicographers want to edit examples, frames, conceptual, or lexical relations this is done by choosing the appropriate tab indicated at the bottom of Figure 1. By clicking one of these tabs, the corresponding panel appears below these tabs. In Figure 1 the panel for *Graph with Hyperonyms and Hyponyms* is displayed.

It is possible to edit the examples and frames associated with a lexical unit via the *Examples and Frames* tab. Frames specify the syntactic valence of a lexical unit. Each frame can have an associated example that indicates a possible usage of the lexical unit for that particular frame. The tab *Examples and Frames* is thus particularly geared towards the editing of verb entries. By clicking on the tab all examples and frames of a lexical unit are listed and can then be modified by choosing the appropriate editing buttons. For more information about these editing functions see Henrich and Hinrichs (2010).

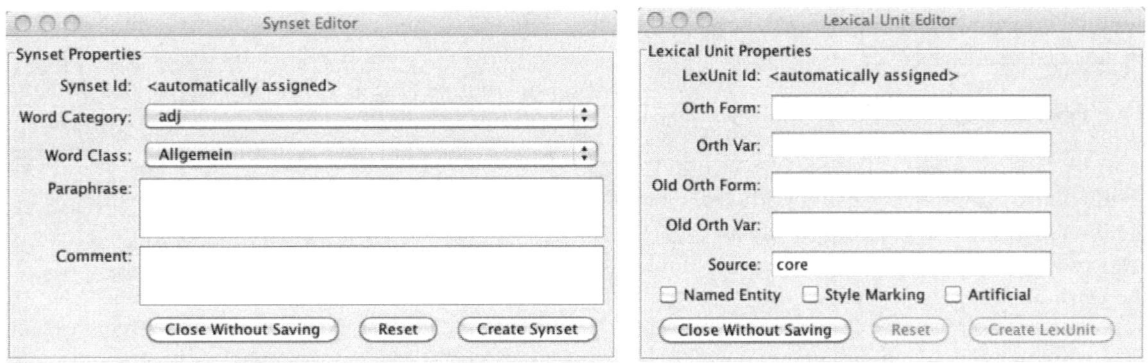

Figure 4. Synset Editor (left). Lexical Units Editor (right).

3.6 Editing of Relations

If lexicographers want to add new conceptual or lexical relations to a synset or a lexical unit this is done by clicking on the *Conceptual Relations Editor* or the *Lexical Relations Editor* shown in Figure 1.

Figure 3 shows the panel that appears if the *Conceptual Relations Editor* has been chosen for the synset containing *Nuss*. To create a new relation, the lexicographer needs to use the buttons *Use as From* and *Use as To* shown in Figure 1. This will insert the ID of the selected synsets from the *Synsets* panel in the corresponding *From* or *To* field in Figure 3. The button *Delete ConRel* allows deletion of a conceptual relation, if all consistency checks are passed.

The *Lexical Relations Editor* tab supports editing all lexical relations. It is not displayed separately for reasons of space, but it is analogue to the *Conceptual Relations Editor* tab for editing conceptual relations.

3.7 Adding Synsets and Lexical Units

The buttons *Add New Hyponym* and *Add New LexUnit* in the *Synsets* panel (see Figure 1) can be used to insert a new synset or lexical unit at the selected place in the GermaNet graph, and the buttons *Delete Synset* and *Delete LexUnit* remove the selected entry, respectively.

The *Synset Editor* in Figure 4 (on the left) shows the window which appears after a click on *Add New Hyponym*. When clicking on the button *Create Synset*, the *Lexical Unit Editor* (shown in Figure 4, right) pops up. This workflow forces the parallel creation of a lexical unit while creating a synset.

3.8 Consistency Checks

GernEdiT facilitates internal consistency of the GermaNet data. This is achieved by the workflow-oriented design of the editor. It is not possible to create a synset without creating a lexical unit in parallel (as described in section 3.7). Furthermore, it is not possible to insert a new synset without specifying the place in the GermaNet hierarchy where the new synset should be added. This is achieved by the button *Add New Hyponym* (see Figure 1) which forces the user to identify the appropriate hyperonym for the new synset to be added. Furthermore, it is not possible to insert a lexical unit without specifying the corresponding synset. On deletion of a synset, all corresponding data such as conceptual relations, lexical units with their lexical relations, frames, and examples, are deleted automatically.

Consistency checks also take effect for the table cell editing in the *Synsets* and *Lexical Units* panels of the main user interface (see Figure 1), e.g., the main orthographic form of a lexical unit may never be empty.

All buttons in GernEdiT are enabled only if the corresponding functionalities meet the consistency requirements, e.g., if a synset consists only of one lexical unit, it is not possible to delete that lexical unit and thus the button *Delete LexUnit* is disabled. Also, if the deletion of a synset or a relation would violate the complete connectedness of the GermaNet graph, it is not possible to delete that synset.

3.9 Further Functionalities

There are further functionalities available through the file menu. Besides retrieving the up-to-date statistics of GermaNet, an editing history makes it possible to list all modifications on the GermaNet data, with the information about who made the change and how the modified item looked before.

GernEdiT supports various export functionalities. For example, it is possible to export all GermaNet contents into XML files, which are used as an exchange format of GermaNet, or to export a list of all verbs with their corresponding frames and examples.

4 Tool Evaluation

In order to assess the usefulness of GernEdiT, we conducted in depth interviews with the GermaNet lexicographers and with the senior researcher who oversees all lexicographic development. At the time of the interview all of these researchers had worked with the tool for about eight months. The present section summarizes the feedback about GernEdiT that was obtained in this way.

The initial learning curve for getting familiar with GernEdiT is considerably lower compared to the learning curve required for the traditional development based on lexicographer files. Moreover, the GermaNet development with GernEdiT is both more efficient and accurate compared to the traditional development along the following dimensions:

1. The menu-driven and graphics-based navigation through the GermaNet graph is much easier compared to finding the correct entry point in the purely text-based format of lexicographer files.
2. Lexicographers no longer need to learn the complex specification syntax of the lexicographer files. Thereby, syntax errors in the specification language – a frequent source of errors prior to development with GernEdiT – are entirely eliminated.
3. GernEdiT facilitates automatic checking of internal consistency and correctness of the GermaNet data such as appropriate linking of lexical units with synsets, connectedness of the synset graph, and automatic closure among relations and their inverse counterparts.
4. It is now even possible to perform further queries, which were not possible before, e.g., listing all hyponyms of a synset.
5. Especially for the senior researcher who is responsible for coordinating the GermaNet lexicographers, it is now much easier to trace back changes and to verify who was responsible for them.
6. The collaborative annotation by several lexicographers working in parallel is now easily possible and does not cause any management overhead as before.

In sum, the lexicographers of GermaNet gave very positive feedback about the use of GernEdiT and also made smaller suggestions for improving its user-friendliness further. This underscores the utility of GernEdiT from a practical point of view.

5 Conclusion and Future Work

In this paper we have described the functionality of GernEdiT. The extremely positive feedback of the GermaNet lexicographers underscores the practical benefits gained by using the GernEdiT tool in practice.

At the moment, GernEdiT is customized for maintaining the GermaNet data. In future work, we plan to adapt the tool so that it can be used with wordnets for other languages as well. This would mean that the wordnet data for a given language would have to be stored in a relational database and that the tool itself can handle the language specific data structures of the wordnet in question.

Acknowledgements

We would like to thank all GermaNet lexicographers for their willingness to experiment with GernEdiT and to be interviewed about their experiences with the tool.

Special thanks go to Reinhild Barkey for her valuable input on both the features and user-friendliness of GernEdiT and to Alexander Kislev for his contributions to the underlying database format.

References

Claudia Kunze and Lothar Lemnitzer. 2002. *GermaNet – representation, visualization, application*. Proceedings of LREC 2002, Main Conference, Vol V. pp. 1485-1491, 2002.

Christiane Fellbaum (ed.). 1998. *WordNet – An Electronic Lexical Database*. Cambridge, MA: MIT Press.

Verena Henrich and Erhard Hinrichs. 2010. *GernEdiT – The GermaNet Editing Tool*. Proceedings of LREC 2010, Main Conference, Valletta, Malta.

Rat für deutsche Rechtschreibung (eds.) (2006). *Deutsche Rechtschreibung – Regeln und Wörterverzeichnis: Amtliche Regelung*. Gunter Narr Verlag Tübingen.

WebLicht: Web-based LRT services for German

Erhard Hinrichs, Marie Hinrichs, Thomas Zastrow
Seminar für Sprachwissenschaft, University of Tübingen
firstname.lastname@uni-tuebingen.de

Abstract

This software demonstration presents WebLicht (short for: *Web-Based Linguistic Chaining Tool*), a web-based service environment for the integration and use of language resources and tools (LRT). WebLicht is being developed as part of the D-SPIN project[1]. WebLicht is implemented as a web application so that there is no need for users to install any software on their own computers or to concern themselves with the technical details involved in building tool chains. The integrated web services are part of a prototypical infrastructure that was developed to facilitate chaining of LRT services. WebLicht allows the integration and use of distributed web services with standardized APIs. The nature of these open and standardized APIs makes it possible to access the web services from nearly any programming language, shell script or workflow engine (UIMA, Gate etc.) Additionally, an application for integration of additional services is available, allowing anyone to contribute his own web service.

1 Introduction

Currently, WebLicht offers LRT services that were developed independently at the Institut für Informatik, Abteilung Automatische Sprachverarbeitung at the University of Leipzig (tokenizer, lemmatizer, co-occurrence extraction, and frequency analyzer), at the Institut für Maschinelle Sprachverarbeitung at the University of Stuttgart (tokenizer, tagger/lemmatizer, German morphological analyser SMOR, constituent and dependency parsers), at the Berlin Brandenburgische Akademie der Wissenschaften (conversion of plain text to D-Spin format, tokenizer, taggers, NE recognizer) and at the Seminar für Sprachwissenschaft/Computerlinguistik at the University of Tübingen (conversion of plain text to D-Spin format, GermaNet, Open Thesaurus synonym service, and Treebank browser). They cover a wide range of linguistic applications, like tokenization, co-occurrence extraction, POS Tagging, lexical and semantic analysis, and several laguages (currently German, English, Italian, French, Romanian, Spanish and Finnish). For some of these tasks, more than one web service is available. As a first external partner, the University of Helsinki in Finnland contributed a set of web services to create morphological annotated text corpora in the Finnish language. With the help of the webbased user interface, these individual web services can be combined into a chain of linguistic applications.

[1] D-SPIN stands for **D**eutsche **SP**rachressourcen **IN**frastruktur; the D-SPIN project is partly financed by the BMBF; it is a national German complement to the EU-project CLARIN. See the URLs http://www.d-spin.org and http://www.clarin.eu for details

2 Service Oriented Architecture

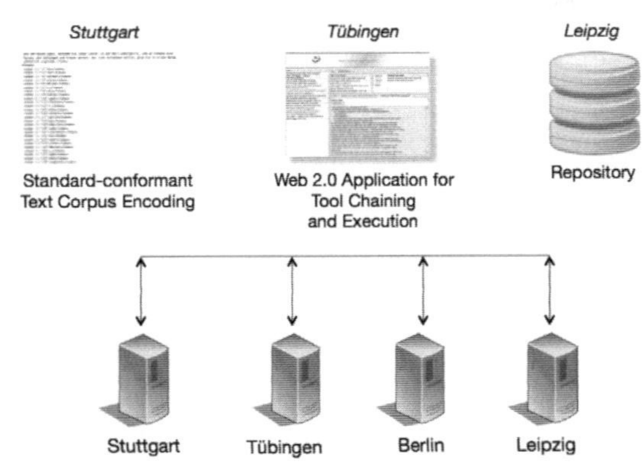

Figure 1: The Overall Structure of WebLicht

WebLicht is a so-called Service Oriented Architecture (Binildas et. al., 2008), which means that distributed and independent services (Tanenbaum et al, 2002) are combined together to a chain of LRT tools. A centralized database, the repository, stores technical and content-related metadata about each service. With the help of

Proceedings of the ACL 2010 System Demonstrations, pages 25–29,
Uppsala, Sweden, 13 July 2010. ©2010 Association for Computational Linguistics

this repository, the chaining mechanism as described in section 3 is implemented. The WebLicht user interface encapsulates this chaining mechanism in an AJAX driven web application. Since web applications can be invoked from any browser, downloading and installation of individual tools on the user's local computer is avoided. But using WebLicht web services is not restricted to the use of the integrated user interface. It is also possible to access the web services from nearly any programming language, shell script or workflow engine (UIMA, Gate etc.). Figure 1 depicts the overall structure of WebLicht.

An important part of Service Oriented Architectures is ensuring interoperability between the underlying services. Interoperability of web services, as they are implemented in WebLicht, refers to the seamless flow of data between them. To be interoperable, these web services must first agree on protocols defining the interaction between the services (WSDL/SOAP, REST, XML-RPC). They must also use a shared and standardized data exchange format, which is preferably based on widely accepted formats already in use (UTF-8, XML). WebLicht uses the RESTstyle API and its own XML-based data exchange format (Text Corpus Format, TCF).

3 The Service Repository

Every tool included in WebLicht is registered in a central repository, located in Leipzig. Also realized as a web service, it offers metadata and processing information about each registered tool. For example, the metadata includes information about the creator, name and the adress of the service. The input and output specifications of each web service are required in order to determine which processing chains are possible.

Combining the metadata and the processing information, the repository is able to offer functions for the chain building process.

Wrappers: TCF, 0.3 / TCF, 0.3	
Inputs	Outputs
lemmas postags -tagset: stts	sem_lex_rels -source: GermaNet

Table 1: Input and Output Specifications of Tübingen's Semantic Annotator

A specialized tool for registering new web services in the repository is available.

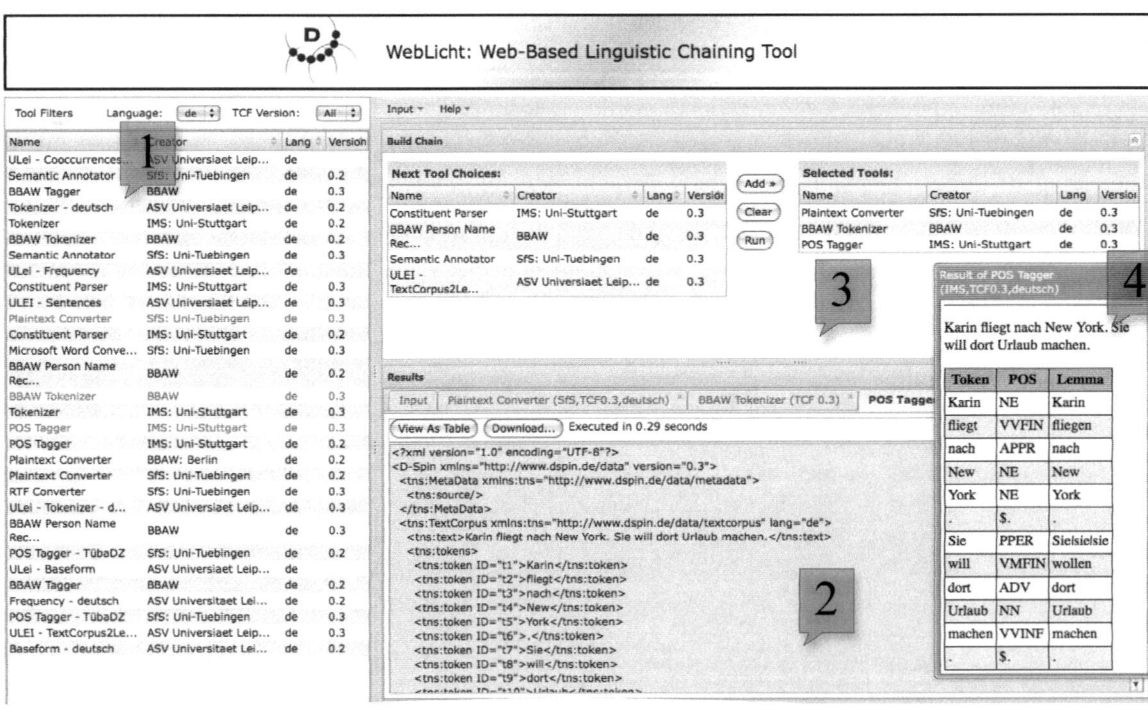

Figure 2: A Screenshot of the WebLicht Webinterface

4 The WebLicht User Interface

Figure 2 shows a screenshot of the WebLicht web interface, developed and hosted in Tübingen. Area 1 shows a list of all WebLicht web services along with a subset of metadata (author, URL, description etc.). This list is extracted on-the-fly from a centralized repository located in Leipzig. This means that after registration in the repository, a web service is immediatley available for inclusion in a processing chain.

The *Language Filter* selection box allows the selection of any language for which tools are available in WebLicht (currently, German, English, Italian, French, Romanian, Spanish or Finnish). The majority of the presently integrated web services operates on German input. The platform, however, is language-independent and supports LRT resources for any language.

Plain text input to the service chain can be specified in one of three ways: a) entered by the user in the *Input tab*, b) file upload from the user's local harddrive or c) selecting one of the sample texts offered by WebLicht (Area 2). Various format converters can be used to convert uploaded files into the data exchange format (TCF) used by WebLicht. Input file formats accepted by WebLicht currently include plain text, Microsoft Word, RTF and PDF.

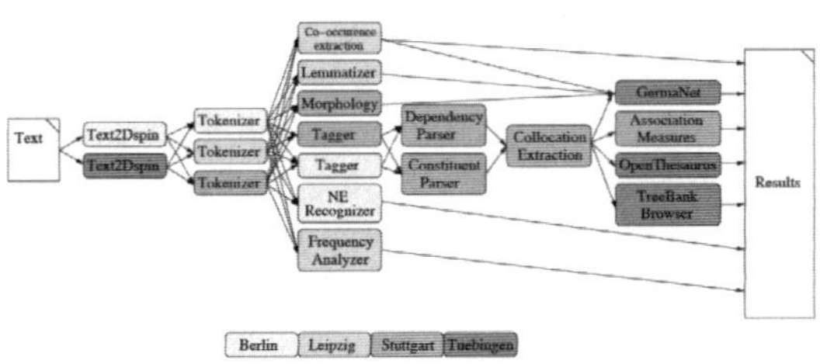

Figure 3: A Choice of Alternative Services

In Area 3, one can assemble the service tool chain and execute it on the input text. The *Selected Tools* list displays all web services that have already been entered into the web service chain. The list under *Next Tool Choices* then offers the set of tools that can be entered as next into the chain. This list is generated by inspecting the metadata of the tools which are already in the chain. The chaining mechanism ensures that this list only contains tools, that are a valid next step in the chain. For example, a Part-of-Speech Tagger can only be added to a chain after a tokenizer has been added. The metadata of each tool contains information about the annotations which are required in the input data and which annotations are added by that tool.

As Figure 3 shows, the user sometimes has a choice of alternative tools - in the example at hand a wide variety of services are offered as candidates. Figure 3 shows a subset of web service workflows currently available in WebLicht. Notice that these workflows can combine tools from various institutions and are not restricted to predefined combinations of tools. This allows users to compare the results of several tool chains and find the best solution for their individual use case.

The final result of running the tool chain as well as each individual step can be visualized in a *Table View* (implemented as a seperate frame, Area 4), or downloaded to the user's local harddrive in WebLicht's own data exchange format TCF.

5 The TCF Format

The D-SPIN *Text Corpus Format* TCF (Heid et al, 2010) is used by WebLicht as an internal data

```
<?xml version="1.0" encoding="UTF-8" ?>
<D-Spin xmlns="http://www.dspin.de/data" version="0.3">
    <tns:MetaData xmlns:tns="http://www.dspin.de/data/metadata">
        <tns:source/>
    </tns:MetaData>
    <tns:TextCorpus xmlns:tns="http://www.dspin.de/data/textcorpus" lang="en">
        <tns:text>Bob went to the zoo.</tns:text>
        <tns:tokens>
            <tns:token ID="t0">Bob</tns:token>
            <tns:token ID="t1">went</tns:token>
            <tns:token ID="t2">to</tns:token>
            <tns:token ID="t3">the</tns:token>
            <tns:token ID="t4">zoo</tns:token>
            <tns:token ID="t5">.</tns:token>
        </tns:tokens>
        <tns:POStags tagset="PennTB">
            <tns:tag tokID="t0">NP</tns:tag>
            <tns:tag tokID="t1">VBD</tns:tag>
            <tns:tag tokID="t2">TO</tns:tag>
            <tns:tag tokID="t3">DT</tns:tag>
            <tns:tag tokID="t4">NN</tns:tag>
            <tns:tag tokID="t5">.</tns:tag>
        </tns:POStags>
        <tns:lemmas>
            <tns:lemma tokID="t0">Bob</tns:lemma>
            <tns:lemma tokID="t1">go</tns:lemma>
            <tns:lemma tokID="t2">to</tns:lemma>
            <tns:lemma tokID="t3">the</tns:lemma>
            <tns:lemma tokID="t4">zoo</tns:lemma>
            <tns:lemma tokID="t5">.</tns:lemma>
        </tns:lemmas>
    </tns:TextCorpus>
</D-Spin>
```

Figure 4: A Short Example of a TCF Document, Containing the Plain Text, Tokens and POS Tags and Lemmas

exchange format. The TCF format allows the combination of the different linguistic annotations produced by the tool chain. It supports incremental enrichment of linguistic annotations at different levels of analysis in a common XML-based format (see Figure 4).

The Text Corpus Format was designed to efficiently enable the seamless flow of data between the individual services of a Service Oriented Architecture.

Figure 4 shows a data sample in the D-SPIN Text Corpus Format. Lexical tokens are identified via token IDs which serve as unique identifiers in different annotation layers. From an organizational point-of-view, tokens can be seen as the central, atomic elements in TCF to which other annotation layers refer. For example, the POS annotations refer to the token IDs in the token annotation layer via the attribute *tokID*. The annotation layers are rendered in a stand-off annotation format. TCF stores all linguistic annotation layers in one single file. That means that during the chaining process, the file grows (see Figure 5). Each tool is permitted to add an arbitrary number of layers, but it is not allowed to change or delete any existing layer.

Within the D-SPIN project, several other XML based data formats were developed beside the TCF format (for example, an encoding for lexicon based data). In order to avoid any confusion of element names between these different formats, namespaces for the different contextual scopes within each format have been introduced.

At the end of the chaining process, converter services will convert the textcorpora from the TCF format into other common and standardized data formats, for example MAF/SynAF or TEI.

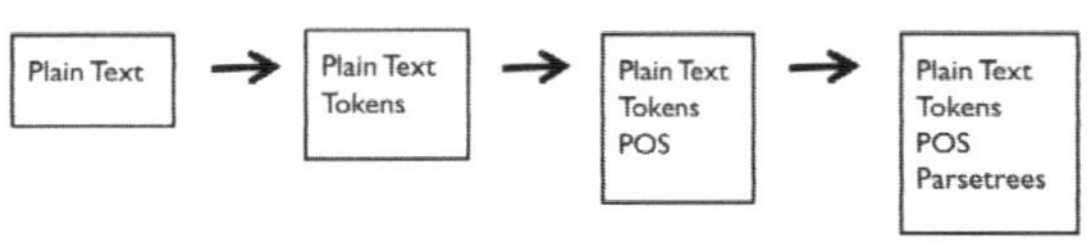

Figure 5: Annotation Layers are Added to the TCF Document by Each Service

6 Implementation Details

The web services are available in RESTstyle and use the TCF data format for input and output. The concrete implementation can use any combination of programming language and server environment.

The repository is a relational database, offering its content also as RESTstyle web services.

The user interface is a Rich Internet Application (RIA), using an AJAX driven toolkit. It incorporates the Java EE 5 technology and can be deployed in any Java application server.

7 How to Participate in WebLicht

Since WebLicht follows the paradigm of a Service Oriented Architecture, it is easily extendable by adding new services. In order to participate in WebLicht by donating additional tools, one must implement the tool as as RESTful web service using the TCF data format. You can find further information including a tutorial on the D-SPIN homepage[2].

8 Further Work

The WebLicht platform in its current form moves the functionality of LRT tools from the users desktop computer into the net (Gray et al, 2005). At this point, the user must download the results of the chaining process and deal with them on his local machine again. In the future, an online workspace has to be implemented so that annotated textcorpora created with WebLicht can also be stored in and retrieved from the net. For that purpose, an integration of the eSciDoc research environment[3] into Weblicht is planned. The eSciDoc infrastructure enables sustainable and reliable long-term preservation of primary research and analysis data.

To make the use of WebLicht more convenient to the end user, there will be predefined processing chains. These will consist of the most commonly used processing chains and will relieve the user of having to define the chains manually.

In the last year, WebLicht has proven to be a realizable and useful service environment for the humanities. In its current state, WebLicht is still a prototype: due to the restrictions of the underlying hardware, WebLicht cannot yet be made available to the general public.

9 Scope of the Software Demonstration

This demonstration will present the core functionalities of WebLicht as well as related modules and applications. The process of building language-specific processing tool chains will be shown. WebLichts capability of offering only appropriate tools at each step in the chain-building process will be demonstrated.

[2] http://weblicht.sfs.uni-tuebingen.de/englisch/weblichttutorial.shtml

[3] For further information about the eSciDoc platform, see https://www.escidoc.org/

The selected tool chain can be applied to any arbitrary uploaded text. The resulting annotated text corpus can be downloaded or visualized using an integrated software module.
All these functions will be shown live using just a webbrowser during the software demonstration.Demo Preview and Hardware Requirements

The call for papers asks submitters of software demonstrations to provide pointers to demo previews and to provide technical details about hardware requirements for the actual demo at the conference.
The WebLicht web application is currently password protected. Access can be granted by requesting an account (weblicht@d-spin.org).
If the software demonstration is accepted, internet access is necessary at the conference, but no special hardware is required. The authors will bring a laptop of their own and if necessary also a beamer.

Acknowledgments

WebLicht is the product of a combined effort within the D-SPIN projects (www.d-spin.org). Currently, partners include: Seminar für Sprachwissenschaft/Computerlinguistik, Universität Tübingen, Abteilung für Automatische Sprachverarbeitung, Universität Leipzig, Institut für Maschinelle Sprachverarbeitung, Universität Stuttgart and Berlin Brandenburgische Akademie der Wissenschaften.

References

Binildas, C.A., Malhar Barai et.al. (2008). *Service Oriented Architectures with Java.* PACKT Publishing, Birmingham – Mumbai

Gray, J., Liu, D., Nieto-Santisteban, M., Szalay, A., DeWitt, D., Heber, G. (2005). Scientific Data Management in the Coming Decade. Technical Report MSR-TR-2005-10, Microsoft Research.

Heid, U., Schmid, H., Eckart, K., Hinrichs, E. (2010). A Corpus Representation Format for Linguistic Web Services: the D_SPIN Text Corpus Format and its Relationship with ISO Standards. In Proceedings of LREC 2010, Malta.

Tanenbaum, A., van Steen, M. (2002). Distributed Systems, Prentice Hall, Upper Saddle River, NJ, 1st Edition.

The S-Space Package: An Open Source Package for Word Space Models

David Jurgens
University of California, Los Angeles,
4732 Boelter Hall
Los Angeles, CA 90095
jurgens@cs.ucla.edu

Keith Stevens
University of California, Los Angeles,
4732 Boelter Hall
Los Angeles, CA 90095
kstevens@cs.ucla.edu

Abstract

We present the S-Space Package, an open source framework for developing and evaluating word space algorithms. The package implements well-known word space algorithms, such as LSA, and provides a comprehensive set of matrix utilities and data structures for extending new or existing models. The package also includes word space benchmarks for evaluation. Both algorithms and libraries are designed for high concurrency and scalability. We demonstrate the efficiency of the reference implementations and also provide their results on six benchmarks.

1 Introduction

Word similarity is an essential part of understanding natural language. Similarity enables meaningful comparisons, entailments, and is a bridge to building and extending rich ontologies for evaluating word semantics. Word space algorithms have been proposed as an automated approach for developing meaningfully comparable semantic representations based on word distributions in text.

Many of the well known algorithms, such as Latent Semantic Analysis (Landauer and Dumais, 1997) and Hyperspace Analogue to Language (Burgess and Lund, 1997), have been shown to approximate human judgements of word similarity in addition to providing computational models for other psychological and linguistic phenomena. More recent approaches have extended this approach to model phenomena such as child language acquisition (Baroni et al., 2007) or semantic priming (Jones et al., 2006). In addition, these models have provided insight in fields outside of linguistics, such as information retrieval, natural language processing and cognitive psychology. For a recent survey of word space approaches and applications, see (Turney and Pantel, 2010).

The parallel development of word space models in different fields has often resulted in duplicated work. The pace of development presents a need for a reliable method for accurate comparisons between new and existing approaches. Furthermore, given the frequent similarity of approaches, we argue that the research community would greatly benefit from a common library and evaluation utilities for word spaces. Therefore, we introduce the **S-Space Package**, an open source framework with four main contributions:

1. reference implementations of frequently cited algorithms
2. a comprehensive, highly concurrent library of tools for building new models
3. an evaluation framework for testing models on standard benchmarks, e.g. the TOEFL Synonym Test (Landauer et al., 1998)
4. a standardized interface for interacting with all word space models, which facilitates word space based applications.

The package is written in Java and defines a standardized Java interface for word space algorithms. While other word space frameworks exist, e.g. (Widdows and Ferraro, 2008), the focus of this framework is to ease the development of new algorithms and the comparison against existing models. Compared to existing frameworks, the S-Space Package supports a much wider variety of algorithms and provides significantly more reusable developer utilities for word spaces, such as tokenizing and filtering, sparse vectors and matrices, specialized data structures, and seamless integration with external programs for dimensionality reduction and clustering. We hope that the release of this framework will greatly facilitate other researchers in their efforts to develop and validate new word space models. The toolkit is available at `http://code.google.com/p/airhead-research/`, which includes a wiki

Proceedings of the ACL 2010 System Demonstrations, pages 30–35,
Uppsala, Sweden, 13 July 2010.

containing detailed information on the algorithms, code documentation and mailing list archives.

2 Word Space Models

Word space models are based on the contextual distribution in which a word occurs. This approach has a long history in linguistics, starting with Firth (1957) and Harris (1968), the latter of whom defined this approach as the Distributional Hypothesis: for two words, their similarity in meaning is predicted by the similarity of the distributions of their co-occurring words. Later models have expanded the notion of co-occurrence but retain the premise that distributional similarity can be used to extract meaningful relationships between words.

Word space algorithms consist of the same core algorithmic steps: word features are extracted from a corpus and the distribution of these features is used as a basis for semantic similarity. Figure 1 illustrates the shared algorithmic structure of all the approaches, which is divided into four components: corpus processing, context selection, feature extraction and global vector space operations.

Corpus processing normalizes the input to create a more uniform set of features on which the algorithm can work. Corpus processing techniques frequently include stemming and filtering of stop words or low-frequency words. For web-gathered corpora, these steps also include removal of non linguistic tokens, such as html markup, or restricting documents to a single language.

Context selection determines which tokens in a document may be considered for features. Common approaches use a lexical distance, syntactic relation, or document co-occurrence to define the context. The various decisions for selecting the context accounts for many differences between otherwise similar approaches.

Feature extraction determines the dimensions of the vector space by selecting which tokens in the context will count as features. Features are commonly word co-occurrences, but more advanced models may perform a statistical analysis to select only those features that best distinguish word meanings. Other models approximate the full set of features to enable better scalability.

Global vector space operations are applied to the entire space once the initial word features have been computed. Common operations include altering feature weights and dimensionality reduction. These operations are designed to improve word similarity by changing the feature space itself.

Document-Based Models
LSA (Landauer and Dumais, 1997)
ESA (Gabrilovich and Markovitch, 2007)
Vector Space Model (Salton et al., 1975)
Co-occurrence Models
HAL (Burgess and Lund, 1997)
COALS (Rohde et al., 2009)
Approximation Models
Random Indexing (Sahlgren et al., 2008)
Reflective Random Indexing (Cohen et al., 2009)
TRI (Jurgens and Stevens, 2009)
BEAGLE (Jones et al., 2006)
Incremental Semantic Analysis (Baroni et al., 2007)
Word Sense Induction Models
Purandare and Pedersen (Purandare and Pedersen, 2004)
HERMIT (Jurgens and Stevens, 2010)

Table 1: Algorithms in the S-Space Package

3 The S-Space Framework

The S-Space framework is designed to be extensible, simple to use, and scalable. We achieve these goals through the use of Java interfaces, reusable word space related data structures, and support for multi-threading. Each word space algorithm is designed to run as a stand alone program and also to be used as a library class.

3.1 Reference Algorithms

The package provides reference implementations for twelve word space algorithms, which are listed in Table 1. Each algorithm is implemented in its own Java package, and all commonalities have been factored out into reusable library classes. The algorithms implement the same Java interface, which provides a consistent abstraction of the four processing stages.

We divide the algorithms into four categories based on their structural similarity: document-based, co-occurrence, approximation, and Word Sense Induction (WSI) models. Document-based models divide a corpus into discrete documents and construct the vector space from word frequencies in the documents. The documents are defined independently of the words that appear in them. Co-occurrence models build the vector space using the distribution of co-occurring words in a context, which is typically defined as a region around a word or paths rooted in a parse tree. The third category of models approximate

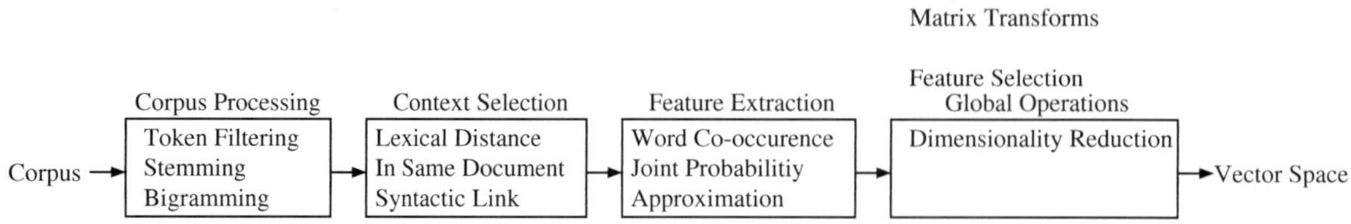

Figure 1: A high-level depiction of common algorithmic steps that convert a corpus into a word space

co-occurrence data rather than model it explicitly in order to achieve better scalability for larger data sets. WSI models also use co-occurrence but also attempt to discover distinct word senses while building the vector space. For example, these algorithms might represent "earth" with two vectors based on its meanings "planet" and "dirt."

3.2 Data Structures and Utilities

The S-Space Package provides efficient implementations for matrices, vectors, and specialized data structures such as multi-maps and tries. Implementations are modeled after the `java.util` library and offer concurrent implementations when multi-threading is required. In addition, the libraries provide support for converting between multiple matrix formats, enabling interaction with external matrix-based programs. The package also provides support for parsing different corpora formats, such as XML or email threads.

3.3 Global Operation Utilities

Many algorithms incorporate dimensionality reduction to smooth their feature data, e.g. (Landauer and Dumais, 1997; Rohde et al., 2009), or to improve efficiency, e.g. (Sahlgren et al., 2008; Jones et al., 2006). The S-Space Package supports two common techniques: the Singular Value Decomposition (SVD) and randomized projections. All matrix data structures are designed to seamlessly integrate with six SVD implementations for maximum portability, including SVDLIBJ[1] , a Java port of SVDLIBC[2], a scalable sparse SVD library. The package also provides a comprehensive library for randomized projections, which project high-dimensional feature data into a lower dimensional space. The library supports both integer-based projections (Kanerva et al., 2000) and Gaussian-based (Jones et al., 2006).

The package supports common matrix transformations that have been applied to word spaces: point wise mutual information (Dekang, 1998), term frequency-inverse document frequency (Salton and Buckley, 1988), and log entropy (Landauer and Dumais, 1997).

3.4 Measurements

The choice of similarity function for the vector space is the least standardized across approaches. Typically the function is empirically chosen based on a performance benchmark and different functions have been shown to provide application specific benefits (Weeds et al., 2004). To facilitate exploration of the similarity function parameter space, the S-Space Package provides support for multiple similarity functions: cosine similarity, Euclidean distance, KL divergence, Jaccard Index, Pearson product-moment correlation, Spearman's rank correlation, and Lin Similarity (Dekang, 1998)

3.5 Clustering

Clustering serves as a tool for building and refining word spaces. WSI algorithms, e.g. (Purandare and Pedersen, 2004), use clustering to discover the different meanings of a word in a corpus. The S-Space Package provides bindings for using the CLUTO clustering package[3]. In addition, the package provides Java implementations of Hierarchical Agglomerative Clustering, Spectral Clustering (Kannan et al., 2004), and the Gap Statistic (Tibshirani et al., 2000).

4 Benchmarks

Word space benchmarks assess the semantic content of the space through analyzing the geometric properties of the space itself. Currently used benchmarks assess the semantics by inspecting the representational similarity of word pairs. Two types of benchmarks are commonly used: word choice tests and association tests. The S-Space Package supports six tests, and has an easily extensible model for adding new tests.

[1] http://bender.unibe.ch/svn/codemap/Archive/svdlibj/

[2] http://tedlab.mit.edu/~dr/SVDLIBC/

[3] http://glaros.dtc.umn.edu/gkhome/views/cluto

		Word Choice			Word Association		
Algorithm	Corpus	TOEFL	ESL	RDWP	R-G	WordSim353	Deese
BEAGLE	TASA	46.03	35.56	46.99	0.431	0.342	0.235
COALS	TASA	65.33	**60.42**	**93.02**	0.572	0.478	**0.388**
HAL	TASA	44.00	20.83	50.00	0.173	0.180	0.318
HAL	Wiki	50.00	31.11	43.44	0.261	0.195	0.042
ISA	TASA	41.33	18.75	33.72	0.245	0.150	0.286
LSA	TASA	56.00[a]	50.00	45.83	0.652	0.519	0.349
LSA	Wiki	60.76	54.17	59.20	**0.681**	**0.614**	0.206
P&P	TASA	34.67	20.83	31.39	0.088	-0.036	0.216
RI	TASA	42.67	27.08	34.88	0.224	0.201	0.211
RI	Wiki	**68.35**	31.25	40.80	0.226	0.315	0.090
RI + Perm.[b]	TASA	52.00	33.33	31.39	0.137	0.260	0.268
RRI	TASA	36.00	22.92	34.88	0.088	0.138	0.109
VSM	TASA	61.33	52.08	84.88	0.496	0.396	0.200

[a] Landauer et al. (1997) report a score of 64.4 for this test, while Rohde et al. (2009) report a score of 53.4.

[b] + Perm indicates that permutations were used with Random Indexing, as described in (Sahlgren et al., 2008)

Table 2: A comparison of the implemented algorithms on common evaluation benchmarks

4.1 Word Choice

Word choice tests provide a target word and a list of options, one of which has the desired relation to the target. Word space models solve these tests by selecting the option whose representation is most similar. Three word choice benchmarks that measure synonymy are supported.

The first test is the widely-reported Test of English as a Foreign Language (TOEFL) synonym test from (Landauer et al., 1998), which consists of 80 multiple-choice questions with four options. The second test comes from the English as a Second Language (ESL) exam and consists of 50 question with four choices (Turney, 2001). The third consists of 200 questions from the Canadian Reader's Digest Word Power (RDWP) (Jarmasz and Szpakowicz, 2003), which unlike the previous two tests, allows the target and options to be multi-word phrases.

4.2 Word Association

Word association tests measure the semantic relatedness of two words by comparing word space similarity with human judgements. Frequently, these tests measure synonymy; however, other types of word relations such as antonymy ("hot" and "cold") or functional relatedness ("doctor" and "hospital") are also possible. The S-Space Package supports three association tests.

The first test uses data gathered by Rubenstein and Goodneough (1965). To measure word similarity, word similarity scores of 51 human reviewers were gathered a set of 65 noun pairs, scored on a scale of 0 to 4. The ratings are then correlated with word space similarity scores.

Finkelstein et al. (2002) test for relatedness. 353 word pairs were rated by either 13 or 16 subjects on a 0 to 10 scale for how related the words are. This test is notably more challenging for word space models because human ratings are not tied to a specific semantic relation.

The third benchmark considers the antonym association. Deese (1964) introduced 39 antonym pairs that Greffenstette (1992) used to assess whether a word space modeled the antonymy relationship. We quantify this relationship by measuring the similarity rank of each word in an antonym pair, w_1, w_2, i.e. w_2 is the kth most-similar word to w_1 in the vector space. The antonym score is calculated as $\frac{2}{rank_{w_1}(w_2)+rank_{w_2}(w_1)}$. The score ranges from $[0, 1]$, where 1 indicates that the most similar neighbors in the space are antonyms. We report the mean score for all 39 antonyms.

5 Algorithm Analysis

The content of a word space is fundamentally dependent upon the corpus used to construct it. Moreover, algorithms which use operations such as the SVD have a limit to the corpora sizes they

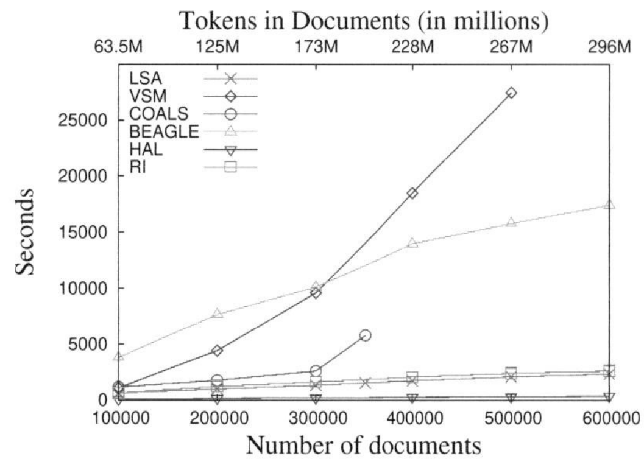

Figure 2: Processing time across different corpus sizes for a word space with the 100,000 most frequent words

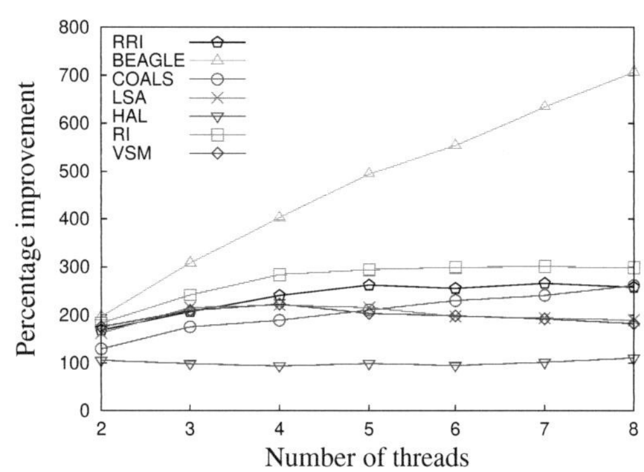

Figure 3: Run time improvement as a factor of increasing the number of threads

can process. We therefore highlight the differences in performance using two corpora. TASA is a collection of 44,486 topical essays introduced in (Landauer and Dumais, 1997). The second corpus is built from a Nov. 11, 2009 Wikipedia snapshot, and filtered to contain only articles with more than 1000 words. The resulting corpus consists of 387,082 documents and 917 million tokens.

Table 2 reports the scores of reference algorithms on the six benchmarks using cosine similarity. The variation in scoring illustrates that different algorithms are more effective at capturing certain semantic relations. We note that scores are likely to change for different parameter configurations of the same algorithm, e.g. token filtering or changing the number of dimensions.

As a second analysis, we report the efficiency of reference implementations by varying the corpus size and number of threads. Figure 2 reports the total amount of time each algorithm needs for processing increasingly larger segments of a web-gathered corpus when using 8 threads. In all cases, only the top 100,000 words were counted as features. Figure 3 reports run time improvements due to multi-threading on the TASA corpus.

Algorithm efficiency is determined by three factors: contention on global statistics, contention on disk I/O, and memory limitations. Multi-threading benefits increase proportionally to the amount of work done per context. Memory limitations account for the largest efficiency constraint, especially as the corpus size and number of features grow. Several algorithms lack data points for larger corpora and show a sharp increase in running time in Figure 2, reflecting the point at which the models no longer fit into 8GB of memory.

6 Future Work and Conclusion

We have described a framework for developing and evaluating word space algorithms. Many well known algorithms are already provided as part of the framework as reference implementations for researches in distributional semantics. We have shown that the provided algorithms and libraries scale appropriately. Last, we motivate further research by illustrating the significant performance differences of the algorithms on six benchmarks.

Future work will be focused on providing support for syntactic features, including dependency parsing as described by (Padó and Lapata, 2007), reference implementations of algorithms that use this information, non-linear dimensionality reduction techniques, and more advanced clustering algorithms.

References

Marco Baroni, Alessandro Lenci, and Luca Onnis. 2007. Isa meets lara: A fully incremental word space model for cognitively plausible simulations of semantic learning. In *Proceedings of the 45th Meeting of the Association for Computational Linguistics*.

Curt Burgess and Kevin Lund. 1997. Modeling parsing constraints with high-dimensional context space. *Language and Cognitive Processes*, 12:177210.

Trevor Cohen, Roger Schvaneveldt, and Dominic Widdows. 2009. Reflective random indexing and indirect inference: A scalable method for discovery of implicit connections. *Journal of Biomedical Informatics*, 43.

J. Deese. 1964. The associative structure of some common english adjectives. *Journal of Verbal Learning and Verbal Behavior*, 3(5):347–357.

Lin Dekang. 1998. Automatic retrieval and clustering of similar words. In *Proceedings of the Joint Annual Meeting of the Association for Computational Linguistics and International Conference on Computational Linguistics*, pages 768–774.

L. Finkelstein, E. Gabrilovich, Y. Matias, E. Z. S. Rivlin, G. Wolfman, and E. Ruppin. 2002. Placing search in context: The concept revisited. *ACM Transactions of Information Systems*, 20(1):116–131.

J. R. Firth, 1957. *A synopsis of linguistic theory 1930-1955*. Oxford: Philological Society. Reprinted in F. R. Palmer (Ed.), (1968). Selected papers of J. R. Firth 1952-1959, London: Longman.

Evgeniy Gabrilovich and Shaul Markovitch. 2007. Computing semantic relatedness using wikipedia-based explicit semantic analysis. In *IJCAI'07: Proceedings of the 20th international joint conference on Artifical intelligence*, pages 1606–1611.

Gregory Grefenstette. 1992. Finding semantic similarity in raw text: The Deese antonyms. In *Working notes of the AAAI Fall Symposium on Probabilistic Approaches to Natural Language*, pages 61–65. AAAI Press.

Zellig Harris. 1968. *Mathematical Structures of Language*. Wiley, New York.

Mario Jarmasz and Stan Szpakowicz. 2003. Roget's thesaurus and semantic similarity. In *Conference on Recent Advances in Natural Language Processing*, pages 212–219.

Michael N. Jones, Walter Kintsch, and Doughlas J. K. Mewhort. 2006. High-dimensional semantic space accounts of priming. *Journal of Memory and Language*, 55:534–552.

David Jurgens and Keith Stevens. 2009. Event detection in blogs using temporal random indexing. In *Proceedings of RANLP 2009: Events in Emerging Text Types Workshop*.

David Jurgens and Keith Stevens. 2010. HERMIT: Flexible Clustering for the SemEval-2 WSI Task. In *Proceedings of the 5th International Workshop on Semantic Evaluations (SemEval-2010)*. Association of Computational Linguistics.

P. Kanerva, J. Kristoferson, and A. Holst. 2000. Random indexing of text samples for latent semantic analysis. In L. R. Gleitman and A. K. Josh, editors, *Proceedings of the 22nd Annual Conference of the Cognitive Science Society*, page 1036.

Ravi Kannan, Santosh Vempala, and Adrian Vetta. 2004. On clusterings: Good, bad and spectral. *Journal of the ACM*, 51(3):497–515.

Thomas K. Landauer and Susan T. Dumais. 1997. A solution to Plato's problem: The Latent Semantic Analysis theory of the acquisition, induction, and representation of knowledge. *Psychological Review*, 104:211–240.

T. K. Landauer, P. W. Foltz, and D. Laham. 1998. Introduction to Latent Semantic Analysis. *Discourse Processes*, (25):259–284.

Sebastian Padó and Mirella Lapata. 2007. Dependency-Based Construction of Semantic Space Models. *Computational Linguistics*, 33(2):161–199.

Amruta Purandare and Ted Pedersen. 2004. Word sense discrimination by clustering contexts in vector and similarity spaces. In *HLT-NAACL 2004 Workshop: Eighth Conference on Computational Natural Language Learning (CoNLL-2004)*, pages 41–48. Association for Computational Linguistics.

Douglas L. T. Rohde, Laura M. Gonnerman, and David C. Plaut. 2009. An improved model of semantic similarity based on lexical co-occurrence. *Cognitive Science*. sumitted.

H. Rubenstein and J. B. Goodenough. 1965. Contextual correlates of synonymy. *Communications of the ACM*, 8:627–633.

M. Sahlgren, A. Holst, and P. Kanerva. 2008. Permutations as a means to encode order in word space. In *Proceedings of the 30th Annual Meeting of the Cognitive Science Society (CogSci'08)*.

G. Salton and C. Buckley. 1988. Term-weighting approaches in automatic text retrieval. *Information Processing & Management*, 24:513–523.

G. Salton, A. Wong, and C. S. Yang. 1975. A vector space model for automatic indexing. *Communications of the ACM*, 18(11):613–620.

Robert Tibshirani, Guenther Walther, and Trevor Hastie. 2000. Estimating the number of clusters in a dataset via the gap statistic. *Journal Royal Statistics Society B*, 63:411–423.

Peter D. Turney and Patrick Pantel. 2010. From Frequency to Meaning: Vector Space Models of Semantics. *Journal of Artificial Intelligence Research*, 37:141–188.

Peter D. Turney. 2001. Mining the Web for synonyms: PMI-IR versus LSA on TOEFL. In *Proceedings of the Twelfth European Conference on Machine Learning (ECML-2001)*, pages 491–502.

Julie Weeds, David Weir, and Diana McCarty. 2004. Characterising measures of lexical distributional similarity. In *Proceedings of the 20th International Conference on Computational Linguistics COLING'04*, pages 1015–1021.

Dominic Widdows and Kathleen Ferraro. 2008. Semantic vectors: a scalable open source package and online technology management application. In *Proceedings of the Sixth International Language Resources and Evaluation (LREC'08)*.

Talking NPCs in a Virtual Game World

Tina Klüwer, Peter Adolphs, Feiyu Xu, Hans Uszkoreit, Xiwen Cheng
Deutsches Forschungszentrum für Künstliche Intelligenz (DFKI)
Projektbüro Berlin
Alt-Moabit 91c
10559 Berlin
Germany
{tina.kluewer,peter.adolphs,feiyu,uszkoreit,xiwen.cheng}@dfki.de

Abstract

This paper describes the *KomParse* system, a natural-language dialog system in the three-dimensional virtual world *Twinity*. In order to fulfill the various communication demands between non-player characters (NPCs) and users in such an online virtual world, the system realizes a flexible and hybrid approach combining knowledge-intensive domain-specific question answering, task-specific and domain-specific dialog with robust chatbot-like chitchat.

1 Introduction

In recent years multi-user online games in virtual worlds such as *Second Life* or *World of Warcraft* have attracted large user communities. Such virtual online game worlds provide new social and economic platforms for people to work and interact in. Furthermore, virtual worlds open new perspectives for research in the social, behavioral, and economic sciences, as well as in human-centered computer science (Bainbridge, 2007). Depending on the game type, non-player characters (NPCs) are often essential for supporting the game plot, for making the artificial world more vivid and ultimately for making it more immersive. In addition, NPCs are useful to populate new worlds by carrying out jobs the user-led characters come in touch with. The range of functions to be filled by NPCs is currently still strongly restricted by their limited capabilities in autonomous acting and communication. This shortcoming creates a strong need for progress in areas such as AI and NLP, especially their planning and dialog systems.

The *KomParse* system, described in this paper, provides NPCs for a virtual online world named *Twinity*, a product of the Berlin startup company *Metaversum*[1]. The *KomParse* NPCs offer various services through conversation with game users using question-answering and dialog functionality. The utilization of Semantic Web technology with RDF-encoded generic and domain-specific ontologies furthermore enables semantic search and inference.

This paper is organized as follows: Section 2 presents the NPC modelling and explains the application scenarios. Section 3 details the knowledge representation and semantic inference in our system. Section 4 explains the system architecture and its key components. Section 5 describes the *KomParse* dialog system. Section 7 gives a conclusion and closes off with our future work.

2 Application Scenario and NPC Modelling

The online game *Twinity* extends the *Second Life* idea by mirroring an urban part of the real world. At the time of this writing, the simulated section of reality already contains 3D models of the cities of Berlin, Singapore and London and it keeps growing. Users can log into the virtual world, where they can meet other users and communicate with them using the integrated chat function or talk to each other via Voice-over-IP. They can style their virtual appearance, can rent or buy their own flats and decorate them as to their preferences and tastes.

Out of many types of NPCs useful for this application such as pedestrians, city guides and personnel in stores, restaurants and bars, we start with two specific characters: a female furniture sales agent and a male bartender. The furniture seller is designed for helping users furnish their virtual apartments. Users can buy pieces of furniture and room decoration from the NPC by describing their demands and wishes in a text chat. During the di-

[1] http://www.metaversum.com/

Proceedings of the ACL 2010 System Demonstrations, pages 36–41,
Uppsala, Sweden, 13 July 2010.

Figure 1: The furniture sales NPC selling a sofa

Figure 2: Our bartender NPC in his bar in *Twinity*

alog with the NPC, the preferred objects are then selected and directly put into a location in the apartment, which can be further refined with the user interfaces that *Twinity* provides.

In the second scenario, the bartender sells virtual drinks. He can talk about cocktails with users, but moreover, he can also entertain his guests by providing trivia-type information about popular celebrities and various relations among them.

We chose these two characters not only because of their value for the *Twinity* application but also for our research goals. They differ in many interesting aspects. First of all, the furniture sales agent is controlled by a complex task model including ontology-driven and data-driven components to guide the conversation. This agent also possesses a much more fine-grained action model, which allows several different actions to cover the potential conversation situations for the selling task. The bartender agent on the other hand is designed not to fulfill one strict task because his clients do not follow a specific goal except ordering drinks. Our bartender has the role of a conversation companion and is able to entertain clients with his broad knowledge. Thus, he is allowed to access to several knowledge bases and is able to handle questions (and later conversations) about a much larger domain called the "gossip domain" which enables conversation about pop stars, movie actors and other celebrities as well as the relations between these people. In order to achieve a high robustness, we integrate a chatbot into the bartender agent to catch chitchat utterances we cannot handle.

3 Knowledge Representation and Semantic Inference

Semantic Web technology is employed for modelling the knowledge of the NPCs. The Resource Description Format (RDF) serves as the base for the actual encoding. An RDF statement is a binary relation instance between two individuals, that is a triple of a predicate and two arguments, called the subject and the object, and written as *subj pred obj* (e.g. `f:Sofa_Alatea f:hasMainColour f:Burgundy`).

All objects and properties the NPC can talk about are modelled in this way. Therefore the knowledge base has to reflect the physical properties of the virtual objects in *Twinity* as faithfully as possible. For instance, specific pieces of furniture are described by their main color, material or style, whereas cocktails are characterized by their ingredients, color, consistence and taste. Furthermore, references to the 3D models of the objects are stored in order to create, find and remove such objects in the virtual world.

The concepts and individuals of the particular domain are structured and organized in domain-specific ontologies. These ontologies are modelled in the Web Ontology Language (OWL). OWL allows us to define concept hierarchies, relations between concepts, domains and ranges of these relations, as well as specific relation instances between instances of a concept. Our ontologies are defined by the freely available ontology editor Protégé 4.0[2]. The advantage of using an ontology for structuring the domain knowledge is

[2] `http://protege.stanford.edu/`, as accessed 27 Oct 2009

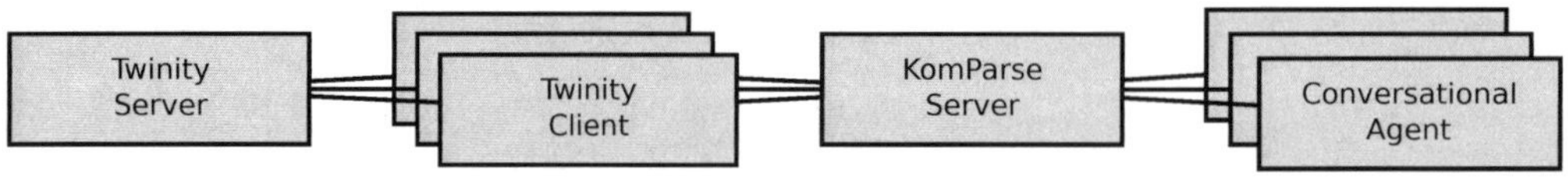

Figure 3: Overall System Architecture – Server/Client Architecture for NPC Control

the modular non-redundant encoding. When combined with a reasoner, only a few statements about an individual have to be asserted explicitely, while the rest can be inferred from the ontology. We employ several ontologies, among which the following are relevant for modelling the specific domains of our NPCs:

- An extensive furniture ontology, created by our project partner ZAS Berlin, defining kinds of furniture, room parts, colors and styles as well as the specific instances of furniture in *Twinity*. This knowledge base contains 95,258 triples, 123 furniture classes, 20 color classes, 243 color instances and various classes defining styles and similar concepts.
- A cocktail ontology, defining 13 cocktail classes with ingredients and tastes in 21,880 triples.
- A biographical ontology, the "gossip ontology", defining biographical and career-specific concepts for people. This ontology is accompanied by a huge database of celebrities, which has been automatically acquired from the Web and covers nearly 600,000 persons and relations between these people like family relationships, marriages and professional relations. (Adolphs et al., 2010)

The furniture ontology is the only knowledge base for the furniture sales agent, whereas the bartender NPC has access to both the cocktail as well as the gossip knowledge base.

We use *SwiftOwlim*[3] for storing and querying the data. *SwiftOwlim* is a "triple store", a kind of database which is specifically built for storing and querying RDF data. It provides a forward-chaining inference engine which evaluates the domain definitions when loading the knowledge repository, and makes implicit knowledge explicit by asserting triples that must also hold true according to the ontology. Once the reasoner is finished, the triple store can be queried directly using the RDF query language SPARQL.

[3] `http://www.ontotext.com/owlim/`

4 Overall System Architecture

Figure 3 shows the overall system architecture. *Twinity* is a server/client application, in which the server hosts the virtual world and coordinates the user interactions. In order to use *Twinity*, users have to download the *Twinity* client. The client allows the user to control the physical representation of the user's character in the virtual world, also called the "avatar". Thus the client is responsible for displaying the graphics, calculating the effects of physical interactions, handling the user's input and synchronizing the 3D data and user actions with the *Twinity* server.

Each NPC comprises two major parts: whereas its avatar is the physical appearance of the NPC in the virtual world, the "conversational agent" provides the actual control logic which controls the avatar autonomously. It is in particular able to hold a conversation with *Twinity* users in that it reacts to a user's presence, interprets user's utterances in dialog context and generates adequate responses.

The *KomParse* server is a multi-client, multi-threaded server written in Java that hosts the conversational agents for the NPCs (section 5). The NPC's avatar, on the other hand, is realized by a modified *Twinity* client. We utilize the Python interface provided by the *Twinity* client to call our own plugin which opens a bidirectional socket connection to the *KomParse* server. The plugin is started together with the *Twinity* client and serves as a mediator between the *Twinity* server and the *KomParse* server from then on (fig. 3). It sends all in-game events relevant to our system to the server and translates the commands sent by the server into *Twinity*-specific actions.

The integration architecture allows us to be maximally independent of the specific game platform. Rather than using the particular programming language and development environment of the platform for realizing the conversational agent or reimplementing a whole client/server protocol for connecting the avatar to the corresponding agent, we use an interface tailored to the specific needs of our system. Thus the *KomParse* system can be naturally extended to other platforms since only the avatar interfaces have to be adapted.

The integration architecture also has the advantage that the necessary services can be easily distributed in a networked multi-platform environment. The *Twinity* clients require a Microsoft Windows machine with a 3D graphics card supporting DirectX 9.0c or higher, 1 GB RAM and a CPU core per instance. The *KomParse* server requires roughly 1 GB RAM. The triple store is run as a separate server process and is accessed by an XML-RPC interface. Roughly 1.2 GB RAM are required for loading our current knowledge base.

5 Conversational Agent: KomParse Dialog System

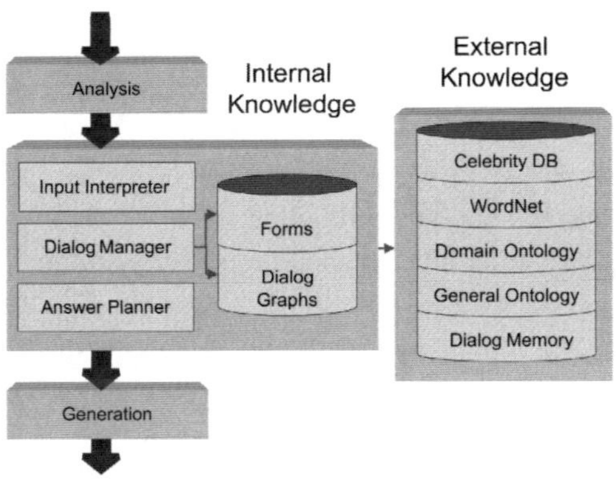

Figure 4: Dialog System: Conversational Agent

The *KomParse* dialog system, the main functionality of the conversational agent, consists of the following three major components: input analyzer, dialog manager and output generator (fig.4).

The *input analyzer* is responsible for the linguistic analysis of the user's textual input including preprocessing such as string cleaning, part-of-speech tagging, named entity recognition, parsing and semantic interpretation. It yields a semantic representation which is the input for the dialog manager.

The *dialog manager* takes the result of the input analyzer and delivers an interpretation based on the dialog context and the available knowledge. It also controls the task conversation chain and handles user requests. The dialog manager determines the next system action based on the interpreted parameters.

The *output generator* realizes the action defined by the dialog manager with its multimodal generation competence. The generated results can be verbal, gestural or a combination of both.

As mentioned above, our dialog system has to deal with two different scenarios. While the focal point of the bartender agent lies in the question answering functionality, the furniture sales agent is driven by a complex dialog task model based on a dialog graph. Thus, the bartender agent relies mainly on question answering technology, in that it needs to understand questions and extract the right answer from our knowledge bases, whereas the sales agent has to accommodate various dialog situations with respect to a sales scenario. It therefore has to understand the dialog acts intended by the user and trigger the corresponding reactions, such as presenting an object, memorizing user preferences, negotiating further sales goals, etc.

The task model for sales conversations is inspired by a corpus resulting from the annotation of a Wizard-of-Oz experiment in the furniture sales agent scenario carried out by our project partner at ZAS (Bertomeu and Benz, 2009). In these experiments, 18 users spent one hour each on furnishing a virtual living room in a *Twinity* apartment by talking to a human wizard controlling the virtual sales agent. The final corpus consists of 18 dialogs containing 3,171 turns with 4,313 utterances and 23,015 alpha-numerical strings (words). The following example shows a typical part of such a conversation:

USR.1:	And do we have a little side table for the TV?
NPC.1:	I could offer you another small table or a sideboard.
USR.2:	Then I'll take a sideboard thats similar to my shelf.
NPC.2:	Let me check if we have something like that.

Table 1: Example Conversation from the Wizard-of-Oz Experiment

The flow of the task-based conversation is controlled by a data-driven finite-state model, which is the backbone of the dialog manager. During a sales conversation, objects and features of objects mentioned by the NPC and the user are extracted from the knowledge bases and added into the underspecified graph nodes and egdes at runtime. This strategy keeps the finite-state graph as small as possible. Discussed objects and their features are stored in a frame-based sub-component named "form". The form contains entries which correspond to ontological concepts in the furniture ontology. During conversation, these entries will be specified with the values of the properties of the discussed objects. This frame-based approach increases the flexibility of the dialog manager (McTear, 2002) and is particularly useful for a task-driven dialog system. As long as the negotiated object is not yet fully specified, the form represents the underspecified object description according to the ontology concept. Every time the user states a new preference or request, the form is enriched with additional features until the set of objects is small enough to be presented to the user for final selection. Thus the actual flow of dialog according to the task model does not have to be expressed by the graph but can be derived on demand from the knowledge and handled by the form which in turn activates the appropriate dialog subgraphs. This combination of graph-based dialog models and form-based task modelling effectively accounts for the interaction of sequential dialog strategies and the non-sequential nature of complex dialog goals.

Given a resolved semantic representation, the dialog manager triggers either a semantic search in the knowledge bases to deliver factual answers as needed in a gossip conversation or a further dialog response for example providing choices for the user in a sales domain. The semantic search is needed in both domains. In case that the semantic representation can neither be resolved in the task domain nor in the gossip domain, it gets passed to the embedded A.L.I.C.E. chatbot that uses its own understanding and generation components (Wallace and Bush, 2001).

5.1 Semantic Representation

The input understanding of the system is implemented as one single understanding pipeline.The understanding pipeline delivers a semantic representation which is the basis for the decision of the dialog manager which action to perform next.

This semantic representation can be extracted from the user input by our understanding component via a robust hybrid approach: either via a number of surface patterns containing regular expressions or via patterns reflecting the syntactic analysis of a dependency parser (de Marneffe and Manning, 2008).

The representation's structure is inspired by our knowledge representation design described in section 3 as well as by predicate logic. The core of the representation is a predicate-argument structure limited to two arguments including message type and the whole syntactic information found by the analysis pipeline. The field "Message Type" can have one of the following values: wh-question, yes/no-question, declarative. Predicates can often be instantiated with the lemmatized matrix verb of the successfully analysed piece of the input. If the input contains a wh-question, the questioned fact is marked as an unfilled argument slot. The general structure can be simplified described as:
<PREDICATE, ARG1, ARG2, [message-type]>

The following examples show the structure used for different input:

- *"Who is the boyfriend of Madonna?"*

  <hasBoyfriend, Madonna, ?, [wh]>

- *"I want to buy a sofa."*

  <buy, I, "a sofa", [declarative]>

5.2 Information Extraction

Both scenarios make use of state-of-the-art information extraction approaches to extract the important pieces from the user input. While the bartender depends on relation extraction to detect the fact or relation questioned by the user (Xu et al., 2007), the sales agent uses information extraction methods to recognize user wishes and demands. As a result, the questioned fact or the demanded object feature equals the ontology structure containing the knowledge needed to handle the user input. The input *"Do you have any red couches?"* for example needs to get processed by the system in such a way that the information regarding the sofa with red color is extracted.

This is done by the system in a data-driven way. The input analysis first tries to find a demanded object in the input via asking the ontology: Every object which can be discussed in the scenario is encoded in the sales agents knowledge base. This can be seen as a Named Entity Recognition step. In case of success, the system tries to detect one of the possible relations of the object found in the input. This is achieved by querying the ontology about what kind of relations the identified object can satisfy. Possible relations are encoded in the class description of the given object. As a result the system can detect a relation "hasColour" for the found object "sofa" and the color value "red". The found information gets inserted into the form which gets more and more similar or if possible equal to a search query via RDF.

Input	Extracted Information	Knowledge Base
Do you have any red couches?	#hasMainColour (#Sofa, #Reds)	{f:Sofa_Alatea f:hasMainColour f:Reds}, {f:Sofa_Franky f:hasMainColour f:Reds}, {...}
I would like a leather one	#hasMaterial(#Sofa, #Leather)	{f:Sofa_Alatea f:hasMaterial f:leather}, {f:Sofa_Franky f:hasMaterial f:leather}, {...}
Who is the boyfriend of Madonna?	#hasBoyfriend(#Madonna, ?)	{f:Madonna f:hasBoyfriend f:GuyRichie}, {f:Madonna f:hasBoyfriend f:VanillaIce}, {...}

Figure 5: Comparison of Input, Extracted Information and Knowledge Base

6 Conclusion and Future Work

The *KomParse* system demonstrates an attractive application area for dialog systems that bears great future potential. Natural language dialog with NPCs is an important factor in making virtual worlds more interesting, interactive and immersive. Virtual worlds with conversing characters will also find many additional applications in education, marketing, and entertainment.

KomParse is an ambitious and nevertheless pragmatic attempt to bring NLP into the world of virtual games. We develop a new strategy to integrate task models and domain ontologies into dialog models. This strategy is useful for task-driven NPCs such as furniture sellers. With the chatty bartender, a combination of task-specific dialog and domain-specific question answering enables a smart wide-domain off-task conversation. Since the online game employs bubble-chat as a mode of communication in addition to Voice-over-IP, we are able to test our dialog system in a real-time application without being hindered by imperfect speech recognition.

The system presented here is still work in progress. The next goals will include various evaluation steps. On the one hand we will focus on single components like hybrid parsing of input utterances and dialog interpretation in terms of precision and recall. On the other hand an evaluation of the two different scenarios regarding the usability are planned in experiments with end users. Moreover we will integrate some opinion mining and sentiment analysis functionality which can be helpful to better detect and understand the user's preferences in the furniture sales agents scenario.

Acknowledgements

The project *KomParse* is funded by the ProFIT programme of the Federal State of Berlin, co-funded by the EFRE programme of the European Union. The research presented here is additionally supported through a grant to the project TAKE, funded by the German Ministry for Education and Research (BMBF, FKZ: 01IW08003). Many thanks go to our project partners at the Centre for General Linguistics (ZAS) in Berlin as well as to the supporting company Metaversum.

References

Peter Adolphs, Xiwen Cheng, Tina Klüwer, Hans Uszkoreit, and Feiyu Xu. 2010. Question answering biographic information and social network powered by the semantic web. In *Proceedings of LREC 2010*, Valletta, Malta.

William Sims Bainbridge. 2007. The scientific research potential of virtual worlds. *Science*, 317.

Nuria Bertomeu and Anton Benz. 2009. Annotation of joint projects and information states in human-npc dialogues. In *Proceedings of the First International Conference on Corpus Linguistics (CILC-09)*, Murcia, Spain.

Marie C. de Marneffe and Christopher D. Manning. 2008. The Stanford typed dependencies representation. In *Coling 2008: Proceedings of the workshop on Cross-Framework and Cross-Domain Parser Evaluation*, Manchester, UK.

Michael F. McTear. 2002. Spoken dialogue technology: enabling the conversational user interface. *ACM Comput. Surv.*, 34(1).

Richard Wallace and Noel Bush. 2001. Artificial intelligence markup language (aiml) version 1.0.1 (2001). Unpublished A.L.I.C.E. AI Foundation Working Draft (rev 006).

Feiyu Xu, Hans Uszkoreit, and Hong Li. 2007. A seed-driven bottom-up machine learning framework for extracting relations of various complexity. In *Proceedings of the 45th Annual Meeting of the Association of Computational Linguistics*, pages 584–591, Prague, Czech Republic, June. Association for Computational Linguistics.

An Open-Source Package for Recognizing Textual Entailment

Milen Kouylekov and Matteo Negri
FBK - Fondazione Bruno Kessler
Via Sommarive 18, 38100 Povo (TN), Italy
[kouylekov,negri]@fbk.eu

Abstract

This paper presents a general-purpose open source package for recognizing Textual Entailment. The system implements a collection of algorithms, providing a configurable framework to quickly set up a working environment to experiment with the RTE task. Fast prototyping of new solutions is also allowed by the possibility to extend its modular architecture. We present the tool as a useful resource to approach the Textual Entailment problem, as an instrument for didactic purposes, and as an opportunity to create a collaborative environment to promote research in the field.

1 Introduction

Textual Entailment (TE) has been proposed as a unifying generic framework for modeling language variability and semantic inference in different Natural Language Processing (NLP) tasks. The Recognizing Textual Entailment (RTE) task (Dagan and Glickman, 2007) consists in deciding, given two text fragments (respectively called *Text - T*, and *Hypothesis - H*), whether the meaning of *H* can be inferred from the meaning of *T*, as in:

T: "Yahoo acquired Overture"
H: "Yahoo owns Overture"

The RTE problem is relevant for many different areas of text processing research, since it represents the core of the semantic-oriented inferences involved in a variety of practical NLP applications including Question Answering, Information Retrieval, Information Extraction, Document Summarization, and Machine Translation. However, in spite of the great potential of integrating RTE into complex NLP architectures, little has been done to actually move from the controlled scenario proposed by the RTE evaluation campaigns[1] to more practical applications. On one side, current RTE technology might not be mature enough to provide reliable components for such integration. Due to the intrinsic complexity of the problem, in fact, state of the art results still show large room for improvement. On the other side, the lack of available tools makes experimentation with the task, and the fast prototyping of new solutions, particularly difficult. To the best of our knowledge, the broad literature describing RTE systems is not accompanied with a corresponding effort on making these systems open-source, or at least freely available. We believe that RTE research would significantly benefit from such availability, since it would allow to quickly set up a working environment for experiments, encourage participation of newcomers, and eventually promote state of the art advances.

The main contribution of this paper is to present the latest release of EDITS (Edit Distance Textual Entailment Suite), a freely available, open source software package for recognizing Textual Entailment. The system has been designed following three basic requirements:

Modularity. System architecture is such that the overall processing task is broken up into major modules. Modules can be composed through a configuration file, and extended as plug-ins according to individual requirements. System's workflow, the behavior of the basic components, and their IO formats are described in a comprehensive documentation available upon download.

Flexibility. The system is general-purpose, and suited for any TE corpus provided in a simple XML format. In addition, both language dependent and language independent configurations are allowed by algorithms that manipulate different representations of the input data.

[1] TAC RTE Challenge: `http://www.nist.gov/tac`
EVALITA TE task: `http://evalita.itc.it`

Proceedings of the ACL 2010 System Demonstrations, pages 42–47,
Uppsala, Sweden, 13 July 2010.

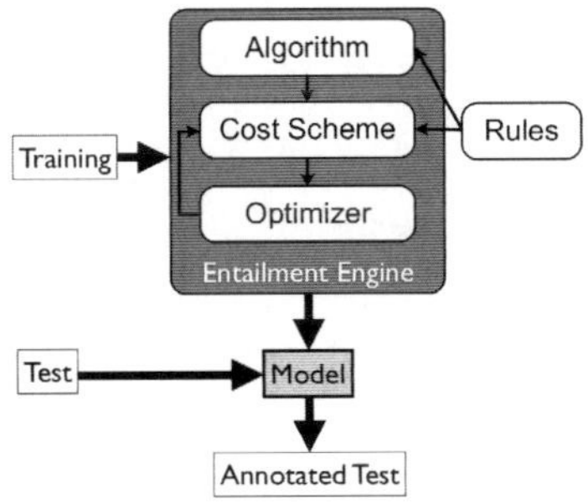

Figure 1: Entailment Engine, main components and workflow

Adaptability. Modules can be tuned over training data to optimize performance along several dimensions (*e.g.* overall Accuracy, Precision/Recall trade-off on YES and NO entailment judgements). In addition, an optimization component based on genetic algorithms is available to automatically set parameters starting from a basic configuration.

EDITS is open source, and available under GNU Lesser General Public Licence (LGPL). The tool is implemented in Java, it runs on Unix-based Operating Systems, and has been tested on MAC OSX, Linux, and Sun Solaris. The latest release of the package can be downloaded from `http://edits.fbk.eu`.

2 System Overview

The EDITS package allows to:

- Create an *Entailment Engine* (Figure 1) by defining its basic components (*i.e.* algorithms, cost schemes, rules, and optimizers);
- Train such *Entailment Engine* over an annotated RTE corpus (containing T-H pairs annotated in terms of entailment) to learn a *Model*;
- Use the *Entailment Engine* and the *Model* to assign an entailment judgement and a confidence score to each pair of an un-annotated test corpus.

EDITS implements a distance-based framework which assumes that the probability of an entailment relation between a given T-H pair is inversely proportional to the *distance* between T and H (*i.e.* the higher the distance, the lower is the probability of entailment). Within this framework the system implements and harmonizes different approaches to distance computation, providing both *edit distance* algorithms, and *similarity* algorithms (see Section 3.1). Each algorithm returns a normalized distance score (a number between 0 and 1). At a training stage, distance scores calculated over annotated T-H pairs are used to estimate a threshold that best separates positive from negative examples. The threshold, which is stored in a *Model*, is used at a test stage to assign an entailment judgement and a confidence score to each test pair.

In the creation of a distance Entailment Engine, algorithms are combined with *cost schemes* (see Section 3.2) that can be *optimized* to determine their behaviour (see Section 3.3), and optional external knowledge represented as *rules* (see Section 3.4). Besides the definition of a single Entailment Engine, a unique feature of EDITS is that it allows for the combination of multiple Entailment Engines in different ways (see Section 4.4).

Pre-defined basic components are already provided with EDITS, allowing to create a variety of entailment engines. Fast prototyping of new solutions is also allowed by the possibility to extend the modular architecture of the system with new algorithms, cost schemes, rules, or plug-ins to new language processing components.

3 Basic Components

This section overviews the main components of a distance Entailment Engine, namely: *i)* algorithms, *iii)* cost schemes, *iii)* the cost optimizer, and *iv)* entailment/contradiction rules.

3.1 Algorithms

Algorithms are used to compute a distance score between T-H pairs.

EDITS provides a set of predefined algorithms, including edit distance algorithms, and similarity algorithms adapted to the proposed distance framework. The choice of the available algorithms is motivated by their large use documented in RTE literature[2].

Edit distance algorithms cast the RTE task as the problem of mapping the whole content of H into the content of T. Mappings are performed as sequences of editing operations (*i.e.* insertion, deletion, substitution of text portions) needed to transform T into H, where each edit operation has a cost associated with it. The distance algorithms available in the current release of the system are:

[2] Detailed descriptions of all the systems participating in the TAC RTE Challenge are available at `http://www.nist.gov/tac/publications`

- Token Edit Distance: a token-based version of the Levenshtein distance algorithm, with edit operations defined over sequences of tokens of T and H;

- Tree Edit Distance: an implementation of the algorithm described in (Zhang and Shasha, 1990), with edit operations defined over single nodes of a syntactic representation of T and H.

Similarity algorithms are adapted to the EDITS distance framework by transforming measures of the lexical/semantic similarity between T and H into distance measures. These algorithms are also adapted to use the three edit operations to support overlap calculation, and define term weights. For instance, substitutable terms in T and H can be treated as equal, and non-overlapping terms can be weighted proportionally to their insertion/deletion costs. Five similarity algorithms are available, namely:

- Word Overlap: computes an overall (distance) score as the proportion of common words in T and H;

- Jaro-Winkler distance: a similarity algorithm between strings, adapted to similarity on words;

- Cosine Similarity: a common vector-based similarity measure;

- Longest Common Subsequence: searches the longest possible sequence of words appearing both in T and H in the same order, normalizing its length by the length of H;

- Jaccard Coefficient: confronts the intersection of words in T and H to their union.

3.2 Cost Schemes

Cost schemes are used to define the cost of each edit operation.

Cost schemes are defined as XML files that explicitly associate a cost (a positive real number) to each edit operation applied to elements of T and H. Elements, referred to as A and B, can be of different types, depending on the algorithm used. For instance, Tree Edit Distance will manipulate *nodes* in a dependency tree representation, whereas Token Edit Distance and similarity algorithms will manipulate *words*. Figure 2 shows an example of

```
<scheme>
  <insertion><cost>10</cost></insertion>
  <deletion><cost>10</cost></deletion>
  <substitution>
    <condition>(equals A B)</condition>
    <cost>0</cost>
  </substitution>
  <substitution>
    <condition>(not (equals A B))</condition>
    <cost>20</cost>
  </substitution>
</scheme>
```

Figure 2: Example of XML Cost Scheme

cost scheme, where edit operation costs are defined as follows:

Insertion(B)=10 - inserting an element B from H to T, no matter what B is, always costs 10;

Deletion(A)=10 - deleting an element A from T, no matter what A is, always costs 10;

substitution(A,B)=0 if A=B - substituting A with B costs 0 if A and B are equal;

substitution(A,B)=20 if A≠B - substituting A with B costs 20 if A and B are different.

In the distance-based framework adopted by EDITS, the interaction between algorithms and cost schemes plays a central role. Given a T-H pair, in fact, the distance score returned by an algorithm directly depends on the cost of the operations applied to transform T into H (edit distance algorithms), or on the cost of mapping words in H with words in T (similarity algorithms). Such interaction determines the overall behaviour of an Entailment Engine, since distance scores returned by the same algorithm with different cost schemes can be considerably different. This allows users to define (and optimize, as explained in Section 3.3) the cost schemes that best suit the RTE data they want to model[3].

EDITS provides two predefined cost schemes:

- Simple Cost Scheme - the one shown in Figure 2, setting fixed costs for each edit operation.

- IDF Cost Scheme - insertion and deletion costs for a word *w* are set to the inverse document frequency of *w* (IDF(*w*)). The substitution cost is set to 0 if a word *w1* from T and a word *w2* from H are the same, and IDF(*w1*)+IDF(*w2*) otherwise.

[3]For instance, when dealing with T-H pairs composed by texts that are much longer than the hypotheses (as in the RTE5 Campaign), setting low deletion costs avoids penalization to short Hs fully contained in the Ts.

In the creation of new cost schemes, users can express edit operation costs, and conditions over the A and B elements, using a meta-language based on a lisp-like syntax (*e.g.* (+ (IDF A) (IDF B)), (not (equals A B))). The system also provides functions to access data stored in hash files. For example, the IDF Cost Scheme accesses the IDF values of the most frequent 100K English words (calculated on the Brown Corpus) stored in a file distributed with the system. Users can create new hash files to collect statistics about words in other languages, or other information to be used inside the cost scheme.

3.3 Cost Optimizer

A cost optimizer is used to adapt cost schemes (either those provided with the system, or new ones defined by the user) to specific datasets.

The optimizer is based on cost adaptation through genetic algorithms, as proposed in (Mehdad, 2009). To this aim, cost schemes can be parametrized by externalizing as parameters the edit operations costs. The optimizer iterates over training data using different values of these parameters until on optimal set is found (*i.e.* the one that best performs on the training set).

3.4 Rules

Rules are used to provide the Entailment Engine with knowledge (*e.g.* lexical, syntactic, semantic) about the probability of entailment or contradiction between elements of T and H. Rules are invoked by cost schemes to influence the cost of substitutions between elements of T and H. Typically, the cost of the substitution between two elements A and B is inversely proportional to the probability that A entails B.

Rules are stored in XML files called Rule Repositories, with the format shown in Figure 3. Each rule consists of three parts: *i)* a left-hand side, *ii)* a right-hand side, *iii)* a probability that the left-hand side entails (or contradicts) the right-hand side.

EDITS provides three predefined sets of lexical entailment rules acquired from lexical resources widely used in RTE: WordNet[4], Lin's word similarity dictionaries[5], and VerbOcean[6].

[4]http://wordnet.princeton.edu

[5]http://webdocs.cs.ualberta.ca/ lindek/downloads.htm

[6]http://demo.patrickpantel.com/Content/verbocean

```
<rule entailment="ENTAILMENT">
  <t>acquire</t>
  <h>own</h>
  <probability>0.95</probability>
</rule>
<rule entailment="CONTRADICTION">
  <t>beautiful</t>
  <h>ugly</h>
  <probability>0.88</probability>
</rule>
```

Figure 3: Example of XML Rule Repository

4 Using the System

This section provides basic information about the use of EDITS, which can be run with commands in a Unix Shell. A complete guide to all the parameters of the main script is available as HTML documentation downloadable with the package.

4.1 Input

The input of the system is an entailment corpus represented in the EDITS Text Annotation Format (ETAF), a simple XML internal annotation format. ETAF is used to represent both the input T-H pairs, and the entailment and contradiction rules. ETAF allows to represent texts at two different levels: *i)* as sequences of tokens with their associated morpho-syntactic properties, or *ii)* as syntactic trees with structural relations among nodes.

Plug-ins for several widely used annotation tools (including TreeTagger, Stanford Parser, and OpenNLP) can be downloaded from the system's website. Users can also extend EDITS by implementing plug-ins to convert the output of other annotation tools in ETAF.

Publicly available RTE corpora (RTE 1-3, and EVALITA 2009), annotated in ETAF at both the annotation levels, are delivered together with the system to be used as first experimental datasets.

4.2 Configuration

The creation of an Entailment Engine is done by defining its basic components (algorithms, cost schemes, optimizer, and rules) through an XML configuration file. The configuration file is divided in modules, each having a set of options. The following XML fragment represents a simple example of configuration file:

```
<module alias="distance">
  <module alias="tree"/>
  <module alias="xml">
    <option name="scheme-file"
```

```
          value="IDF_Scheme.xml"/>
  </module>
  <module alias="pso"/>
</module>
```

This configuration defines a distance Entailment Engine that combines Tree Edit Distance as a core distance algorithm, and the predefined IDF Cost Scheme that will be optimized on training data with the Particle Swarm Optimization algorithm ("*pso*") as in (Mehdad, 2009). Adding external knowledge to an entailment engine can be done by extending the configuration file with a reference to a rules file (*e.g.* "*rules.xml*") as follows:

```
  <module alias="rules">
    <option name="rules-file"
            value="rules.xml"/>
  </module>
```

4.3 Training and Test

Given a configuration file and an RTE corpus annotated in ETAF, the user can run the **training** procedure to learn a model. At this stage, EDITS allows to tune performance along several dimensions (*e.g.* overall Accuracy, Precision/Recall trade-off on YES and/or NO entailment judgements). By default the system maximizes the overall accuracy (distinction between YES and NO pairs). The output of the training phase is a *model*: a zip file that contains the learned threshold, the configuration file, the cost scheme, and the entailment/contradiction rules used to calculate the threshold. The explicit availability of all this information in the model allows users to share, replicate and modify experiments[7].

Given a model and an un-annotated RTE corpus as input, the **test** procedure produces a file containing for each pair: *i)* the decision of the system (YES, NO), *ii)* the confidence of the decision, *iii)* the entailment score, *iv)* the sequence of edit operations made to calculate the entailment score.

4.4 Combining Engines

A relevant feature of EDITS is the possibility to combine multiple Entailment Engines into a single one. This can be done by grouping their definitions as sub-modules in the configuration file. EDITS allows users to define customized combination strategies, or to use two predefined combination modalities provided with the package,

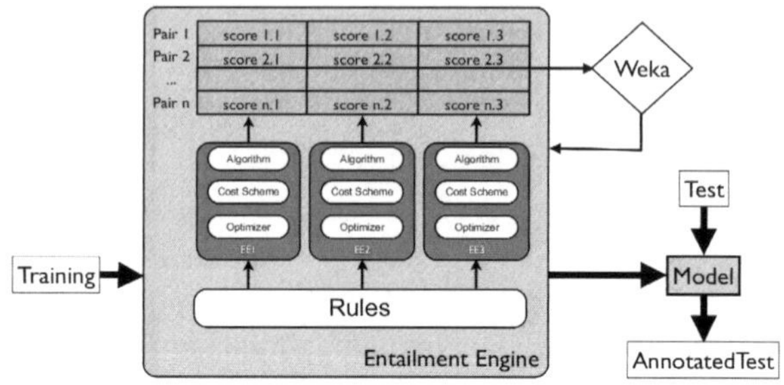

Figure 4: Combined Entailment Engines

namely: *i)* Linear Combination, and *ii)* Classifier Combination. The two modalities combine in different ways the entailment scores produced by multiple independent engines, and return a final decision for each T-H pair.

Linear Combination returns an overall entailment score as the weighted sum of the entailment scores returned by each engine:

$$score_{combination} = \sum_{i=0}^{n} score_i * weight_i \quad (1)$$

In this formula, $weight_i$ is an ad-hoc weight parameter for each entailment engine. Optimal weight parameters can be determined using the same optimization strategy used to optimize the cost schemes, as described in Section 3.3.

Classifier Combination is similar to the approach proposed in (Malakasiotis and Androutsopoulos, 2007), and is based on using the entailment scores returned by each engine as features to train a classifier (see Figure 4). To this aim, EDITS provides a plug-in that uses the Weka[8] machine learning workbench as a core. By default the plug-in uses an SVM classifier, but other Weka algorithms can be specified as options in the configuration file.

The following configuration file describes a combination of two engines (*i.e.* one based on Tree Edit Distance, the other based on Cosine Similarity), used to train a classifier with Weka[9].

```
<module alias="weka">
  <module alias="distance">
    <module alias="tree"/>
    <module alias="xml">
      <option name="scheme-file"
              value="IDF_Scheme.xml"/>
    </module>
  </module>
```

[7] Our policy is to publish online the models we use for participation in the RTE Challenges. We encourage other users of EDITS to do the same, thus creating a collaborative environment, allow new users to quickly modify working configurations, and replicate results.

[8] http://www.cs.waikato.ac.nz/ml/weka

[9] A linear combination can be easily obtained by changing the alias of the highest-level module ("weka") into "linear".

```
  <module alias="distance">
    <module alias="cosine"/>
    <module alias="IDF_Scheme.xml"/>
  </module>
</module>
```

5 Experiments with EDITS

To give an idea of the potentialities of the EDITS package in terms of flexibility and adaptability, this section reports some results achieved in RTE-related tasks by previous versions of the tool. The system has been tested in different scenarios, ranging from the evaluation of standalone systems within task-specific RTE Challenges, to their integration in more complex architectures.

As regards the RTE Challenges, in the last years EDITS has been used to participate both in the PASCAL/TAC RTE Campaigns for the English language (Mehdad et al., 2009), and in the EVALITA RTE task for Italian (Cabrio et al., 2009). In the last RTE-5 Campaign the result achieved in the traditional "2-way Main task" (60.17% Accuracy) roughly corresponds to the performance of the average participating systems (60.36%). In the "Search" task (which consists in finding all the sentences that entail a given H in a given set of documents about a topic) the same configuration achieved an F1 of 33.44%, ranking 3rd out of eight participants (average score 29.17% F1). In the EVALITA 2009 RTE task, EDITS ranked first with an overall 71.0% Accuracy. To promote the use of EDITS and ease experimentation, the complete models used to produce each submitted run can be downloaded with the system. An improved model obtained with the current release of EDITS, and trained over RTE-5 data (61.83% Accuracy on the "2-way Main task" test set), is also available upon download.

As regards application-oriented integrations, EDITS has been successfully used as a core component in a Restricted-Domain Question Answering system within the EU-Funded QALL-ME Project[10]. Within this project, an entailment-based approach to Relation Extraction has been defined as the task of checking for the existence of entailment relations between an input question (the *text* in RTE parlance), and a set of textual realizations of domain-specific binary relations (the *hypotheses* in RTE parlance). In recognizing 14 relations relevant in the CINEMA domain present in a collection of spoken English requests, the system achieved an F1 of 72.9%, allowing to return correct answers to 83% of 400 test questions (Negri and Kouylekov, 2009).

[10]http://qallme.fbk.eu

6 Conclusion

We have presented the first open source package for recognizing Textual Entailment. The system offers a modular, flexible, and adaptable working environment to experiment with the task. In addition, the availability of pre-defined system configurations, tested in the past Evaluation Campaigns, represents a first contribution to set up a collaborative environment, and promote advances in RTE research. Current activities are focusing on the development of a Graphical User Interface, to further simplify the use of the system.

Acknowledgments

The research leading to these results has received funding from the European Community's Seventh Framework Programme (FP7/2007-2013) under Grant Agreement n. 248531 (CoSyne project).

References

Prodromos Malakasiotis and Ion Androutsopoulos 2007. *Learning Textual Entailment using SVMs and String Similarity Measures*. Proc. of the ACL '07 Workshop on Textual Entailment and Paraphrasing.

Ido Dagan and 0ren Glickman 2004. *Probabilistic Textual Entailment: Generic Applied Modeling of Language Variability*. Proc. of the PASCAL Workshop on Learning Methods for Text Understanding and Mining.

Kaizhong Zhang and Dennis Shasha 1990. *Fast Algorithm for the Unit Cost Editing Distance Between Trees*. Journal of Algorithms. vol.11.

Yashar Mehdad 2009. *Automatic Cost Estimation for Tree Edit Distance Using Particle Swarm Optimization*. Proc. of ACL-IJCNLP 2009.

Matteo Negri and Milen Kouylekov 2009. *Question Answering over Structured Data: an Entailment-Based Approach to Question Analysis*. Proc. of RANLP-2009.

Elena Cabrio, Yashar Mehdad, Matteo Negri, Milen Kouylekov, and Bernardo Magnini 2009. *Recognizing Textual Entailment for Italian EDITS @ EVALITA 2009* Proc. of EVALITA 2009.

Yashar Mehdad, Matteo Negri, Elena Cabrio, Milen Kouylekov, and Bernardo Magnini 2009. *Recognizing Textual Entailment for English EDITS @ TAC 2009* To appear in Proceedings of TAC 2009.

Personalising speech-to-speech translation in the EMIME project

Mikko Kurimo[1†], William Byrne[6], John Dines[3], Philip N. Garner[3], Matthew Gibson[6], Yong Guan[5], Teemu Hirsimäki[1], Reima Karhila[1], Simon King[2], Hui Liang[3], Keiichiro Oura[4], Lakshmi Saheer[3], Matt Shannon[6], Sayaka Shiota[4], Jilei Tian[5], Keiichi Tokuda[4], Mirjam Wester[2], Yi-Jian Wu[4], Junichi Yamagishi[2]

[1] Aalto University, Finland, [2] University of Edinburgh, UK, [3] Idiap Research Institute, Switzerland, [4] Nagoya Institute of Technology, Japan, [5] Nokia Research Center Beijing, China, [6] University of Cambridge, UK

[†]Corresponding author: Mikko.Kurimo@tkk.fi

Abstract

In the EMIME project we have studied unsupervised cross-lingual speaker adaptation. We have employed an HMM statistical framework for both speech recognition and synthesis which provides transformation mechanisms to adapt the synthesized voice in TTS (text-to-speech) using the recognized voice in ASR (automatic speech recognition). An important application for this research is personalised speech-to-speech translation that will use the voice of the speaker in the input language to utter the translated sentences in the output language. In mobile environments this enhances the users' interaction across language barriers by making the output speech sound more like the original speaker's way of speaking, even if she or he could not speak the output language.

1 Introduction

A mobile real-time speech-to-speech translation (S2ST) device is one of the grand challenges in natural language processing (NLP). It involves several important NLP research areas: automatic speech recognition (ASR), statistical machine translation (SMT) and speech synthesis, also known as text-to-speech (TTS). In recent years significant advance have also been made in relevant technological devices: the size of powerful computers has decreased to fit in a mobile phone and fast WiFi and 3G networks have spread widely to connect them to even more powerful computation servers. Several hand-held S2ST applications and devices have already become available, for example by IBM, Google or Jibbigo[1], but there are still serious limitations in vocabulary and language selection and performance.

When an S2ST device is used in practical human interaction across a language barrier, one feature that is often missed is the personalization of the output voice. Whoever speaks to the device in what ever manner, the output voice always sounds the same. Producing high-quality synthesis voices is expensive and even if the system had many output voices, it is hard to select one that would sound like the input voice. There are many features in the output voice that could raise the interaction experience to a much more natural level, for example, emotions, speaking rate, loudness and the speaker identity.

After the recent development in hidden Markov model (HMM) based TTS, it has become possible to adapt the output voice using model transformations that can be estimated from a small number of speech samples. These techniques, for instance the maximum likelihood linear regression (MLLR), are adopted from HMM-based ASR where they are very powerful in fast adaptation of speaker and recording environment characteristics (Gales, 1998). Using hierarchical regression trees, the TTS and ASR models can further be coupled in a way that enables unsupervised TTS adaptation (King et al., 2008). In unsupervised adaptation samples are annotated by applying ASR. By eliminating the need for human intervention it becomes possible to perform voice adaptation for TTS in almost real-time.

The target in the EMIME project[2] is to study unsupervised cross-lingual speaker adaptation for S2ST systems. The first results of the project have

[1]http://www.jibbigo.com

[2]http://emime.org

Proceedings of the ACL 2010 System Demonstrations, pages 48–53,
Uppsala, Sweden, 13 July 2010. ©2010 Association for Computational Linguistics

been, for example, to bridge the gap between the ASR and TTS (Dines et al., 2009), to improve the baseline ASR (Hirsimäki et al., 2009) and SMT (de Gispert et al., 2009) systems for morphologically rich languages, and to develop robust TTS (Yamagishi et al., 2010). The next step has been preliminary experiments in intra-lingual and cross-lingual speaker adaptation (Wu et al., 2008). For cross-lingual adaptation several new methods have been proposed for mapping the HMM states, adaptation data and model transformations (Wu et al., 2009).

In this presentation we can demonstrate the various new results in ASR, SMT and TTS. Even though the project is still ongoing, we have an initial version of mobile S2ST system and cross-lingual speaker adaptation to show.

2 Baseline ASR, TTS and SMT systems

The baseline ASR systems in the project are developed using the HTK toolkit (Young et al., 2001) for Finnish, English, Mandarin and Japanese. The systems can also utilize various real-time decoders such as Julius (Kawahara et al., 2000), Juicer at IDIAP and the TKK decoder (Hirsimäki et al., 2006). The main structure of the baseline systems for each of the four languages is similar and fairly standard and in line with most other state-of-the-art large vocabulary ASR systems. Some special flavors for have been added, such as the morphological analysis for Finnish (Hirsimäki et al., 2009). For speaker adaptation, the MLLR transformation based on hierarchical regression classes is included for all languages.

The baseline TTS systems in the project utilize the HTS toolkit (Yamagishi et al., 2009) which is built on top of the HTK framework. The HMM-based TTS systems have been developed for Finnish, English, Mandarin and Japanese. The systems include an average voice model for each language trained over hundreds of speakers taken from standard ASR corpora, such as Speecon (Iskra et al., 2002). Using speaker adaptation transforms, thousands of new voices have been created (Yamagishi et al., 2010) and new voices can be added using a small number of either supervised or unsupervised speech samples. Cross-lingual adaptation is possible by creating a mapping between the HMM states in the input and the output language (Wu et al., 2009).

Because the resources of the EMIME project have been focused on ASR, TTS and speaker adaptation, we aim at relying on existing solutions for SMT as far as possible. New methods have been studied concerning the morphologically rich languages (de Gispert et al., 2009), but for the S2ST system we are currently using Google translate[3].

3 Demonstrations to show

3.1 Monolingual systems

In robust speech synthesis, a computer can learn to speak in the desired way after processing only a relatively small amount of training speech. The training speech can even be a normal quality recording outside the studio environment, where the target speaker is speaking to a standard microphone and the speech is not annotated. This differs dramatically from conventional TTS, where building a new voice requires an hour or more careful repetition of specially selected prompts recorded in an anechoic chamber with high quality equipment.

Robust TTS has recently become possible using the statistical HMM framework for both ASR and TTS. This framework enables the use of efficient speaker adaptation transformations developed for ASR to be used also for the TTS models. Using large corpora collected for ASR, we can train average voice models for both ASR and TTS. The training data may include a small amount of speech with poor coverage of phonetic contexts from each single speaker, but by summing the material over hundreds of speakers, we can obtain sufficient models for an average speaker. Only a small amount of adaptation data is then required to create transformations for tuning the average voice closer to the target voice.

In addition to the supervised adaptation using annotated speech, it is also possible to employ ASR to create annotations. This unsupervised adaptation enables the system to use a much broader selection of sources, for example, recorded samples from the internet, to learn a new voice.

The following systems will demonstrate the results of monolingual adaptation:

1. In *EMIME Voice cloning in Finnish and English* the goal is that the users can clone their own voice. The user will dictate for about

[3]`http://translate.google.com`

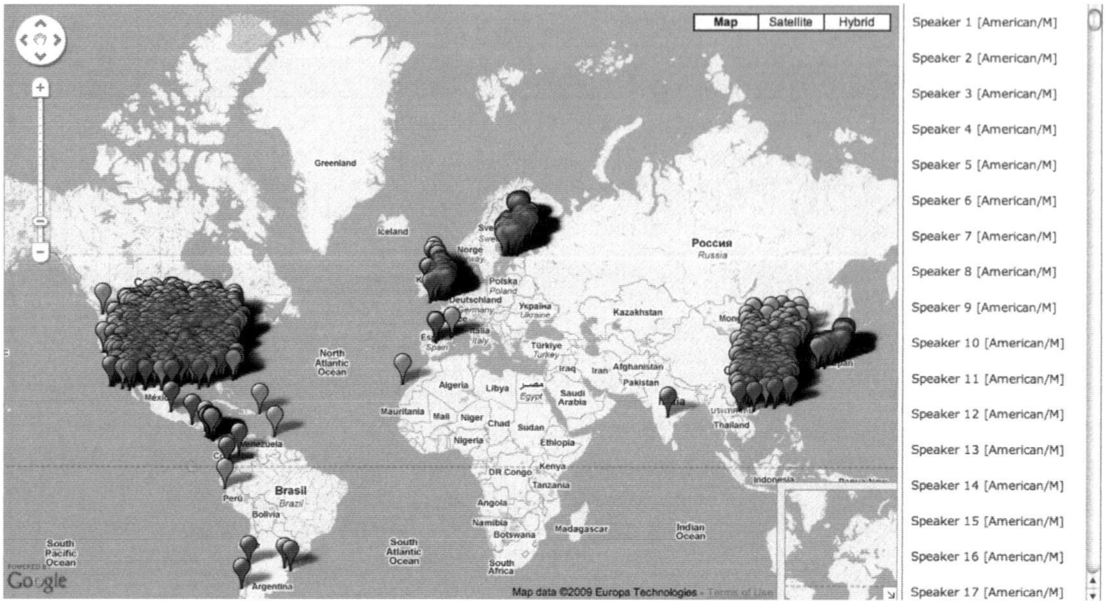

Figure 1: Geographical representation of HTS voices trained on ASR corpora for EMIME projects. Blue markers show male speakers and red markers show female speakers. Available online via http://www.emime.org/learn/speech-synthesis/listen/Examples-for-D2.1

10 minutes and then after half an hour of processing time, the TTS system has transformed the average model towards the user's voice and can speak with this voice. The cloned voices may become especially valuable, for example, if a person's voice is later damaged in an accident or by a disease.

2. In *EMIME Thousand voices map* the goal is to browse the world's largest collection of synthetic voices by using a world map interface (Yamagishi et al., 2010). The user can zoom in the world map and select any voice, which are organized according to the place of living of the adapted speaker, to utter the given sentence. This interactive geographical representation is shown in Figure 1. Each marker corresponds to an individual speaker. Blue markers show male speakers and red markers show female speakers. Some markers are in arbitrary locations (in the correct country) because precise location information is not available for all speakers. This geographical representation, which includes an interactive TTS demonstration of many of the voices, is available from the URL provided. Clicking on a marker will play synthetic speech from that speaker[4]. As well as being a convenient interface to compare the many voices, the interactive map is an attractive and easy-to-understand demonstration of the technology being developed in EMIME.

3. The models developed in the HMM framework can be demonstrated also in adaptation of an ASR system for *large-vocabulary continuous speech recognition*. By utilizing morpheme-based language models instead of word-based models the Finnish ASR system is able to cover practically an unlimited vocabulary (Hirsimäki et al., 2006). This is necessary for morphologically rich languages where, due to inflection, derivation and composition, there exists so many different word forms that word based language modeling becomes impractical.

3.2 Cross-lingual systems

In the EMIME project the goal is to learn cross-lingual speaker adaptation. Here the output language ASR or TTS system is adapted from speech samples in the input language. The results so far are encouraging, especially for TTS: Even though the cross-lingual adaptation may somewhat degrade the synthesis quality, the adapted speech now sounds more like the target speaker. Several recent evaluations of the cross-lingual speaker

[4]Currently the interactive mode supports English and Spanish only. For other languages this only provides presynthesised examples, but we plan to add an interactive type-in text-to-speech feature in the near future.

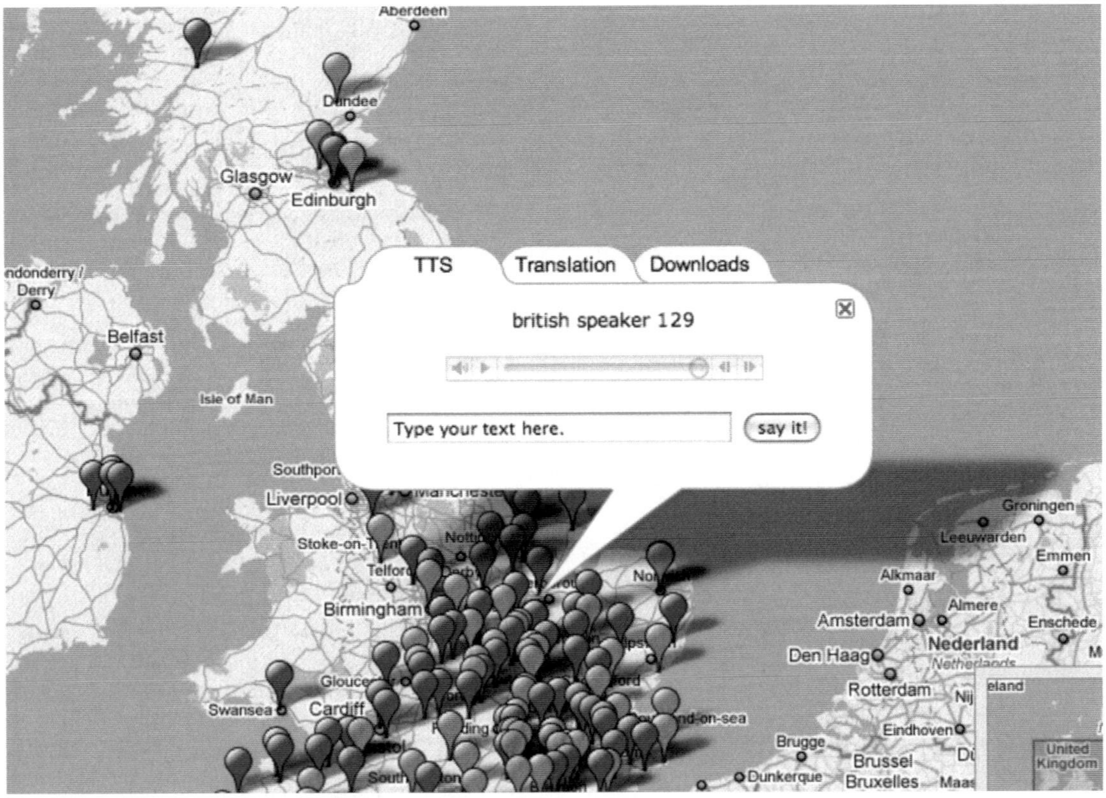

Figure 2: All English HTS voices can be used as online TTS on the geographical map.

adaptation methods can be found in (Gibson et al., 2010; Oura et al., 2010; Liang et al., 2010; Oura et al., 2009).

The following systems have been created to demonstrate cross-lingual adaptation:

1. In *EMIME Cross-lingual Finnish/English and Mandarin/English TTS adaptation* the input language sentences dictated by the user will be used to learn the characteristics of her or his voice. The adapted cross-lingual model will be used to speak output language (English) sentences in the user's voice. The user does not need to be bilingual and only reads sentences in their native language.

2. In *EMIME Real-time speech-to-speech mobile translation demo* two users will interact using a pair of mobile N97 devices (see Figure 3). The system will recognize the phrase the other user is speaking in his native language and translate and speak it in the native language of the other user. After a few sentences the system will have the speaker adaptation transformations ready and can apply them in the synthesized voices to make them sound more like the original speaker instead of a standard voice. The first real-time demo version is available for the Mandarin/English language pair.

3. *The morpheme-based translation system* for Finnish/English and English/Finnish can be compared to a word based translation for arbitrary sentences. The morpheme-based approach is particularly useful for language pairs where one or both languages are morphologically rich ones where the amount and complexity of different word forms severely limits the performance for word-based translation. The morpheme-based systems can learn translation models for phrases where morphemes are used instead of words (de Gispert et al., 2009). Recent evaluations (Kurimo et al., 2009) have shown that the performance of the unsupervised data-driven morpheme segmentation can rival the conventional rule-based ones. This is very useful if hand-crafted morphological analyzers are not available or their coverage is not sufficient for all languages.

Acknowledgments

The research leading to these results was partly funded from the European Communitys Seventh

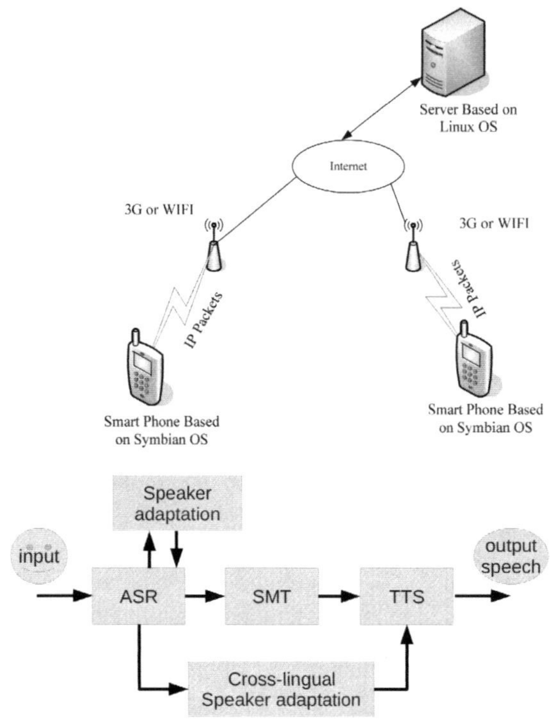

Figure 3: EMIME Real-time speech-to-speech mobile translation demo

Framework Programme (FP7/2007-2013) under grant agreement 213845 (the EMIME project).

References

A. de Gispert, S. Virpioja, M. Kurimo, and W. Byrne. 2009. Minimum Bayes risk combination of translation hypotheses from alternative morphological decompositions. In *Proc. NAACL-HLT*.

J. Dines, J. Yamagishi, and S. King. 2009. Measuring the gap between HMM-based ASR and TTS. In *Proc. Interspeech '09*, Brighton, UK.

M. Gales. 1998. Maximum likelihood linear transformations for HMM-based speech recognition. *Computer Speech and Language*, 12(2):75–98.

M. Gibson, T. Hirsimäki, R. Karhila, M. Kurimo, and W. Byrne. 2010. Unsupervised cross-lingual speaker adaptation for HMM-based speech synthesis using two-pass decision tree construction. In *Proc. of ICASSP*, page to appear, March.

T. Hirsimäki, M. Creutz, V. Siivola, M. Kurimo, S. Virpioja, and J. Pylkkönen. 2006. Unlimited vocabulary speech recognition with morph language models applied to finnish. *Computer Speech & Language*, 20(4):515–541, October.

T. Hirsimäki, J. Pylkkönen, and M Kurimo. 2009. Importance of high-order n-gram models in morph-based speech recognition. *IEEE Trans. Audio, Speech, and Language Process.*, 17:724–732.

D. Iskra, B. Grosskopf, K. Marasek, H. van den Heuvel, F. Diehl, and A. Kiessling. 2002. SPEECON speech databases for consumer devices: Database specification and validation. In *Proc. LREC*, pages 329–333.

T. Kawahara, A. Lee, T. Kobayashi, K. Takeda, N. Minematsu, S. Sagayama, K. Itou, A. Ito, M. Yamamoto, A. Yamada, T. Utsuro, and K. Shikano. 2000. Free software toolkit for japanese large vocabulary continuous speech recognition. In *Proc. ICSLP-2000*, volume 4, pages 476–479.

S. King, K. Tokuda, H. Zen, and J. Yamagishi. 2008. Unsupervised adaptation for HMM-based speech synthesis. In *Proc. Interspeech 2008*, pages 1869–1872, September.

Mikko Kurimo, Sami Virpioja, Ville T. Turunen, Graeme W. Blackwood, and William Byrne. 2009. Overview and results of Morpho Challenge 2009. In *Working Notes for the CLEF 2009 Workshop*, Corfu, Greece, September.

H. Liang, J. Dines, and L. Saheer. 2010. A comparison of supervised and unsupervised cross-lingual speaker adaptation approaches for HMM-based speech synthesis. In *Proc. of ICASSP*, page to appear, March.

Keiichiro Oura, Junichi Yamagishi, Simon King, Mirjam Wester, and Keiichi Tokuda. 2009. Unsupervised speaker adaptation for speech-to-speech translation system. In *Proc. SLP (Spoken Language Processing)*, number 356 in 109, pages 13–18.

K. Oura, K. Tokuda, J. Yamagishi, S. King, and M. Wester. 2010. Unsupervised cross-lingual speaker adaptation for HMM-based speech synthesis. In *Proc. of ICASSP*, page to appear, March.

Y.-J. Wu, S. King, and K. Tokuda. 2008. Cross-lingual speaker adaptation for HMM-based speech synthesis. In *Proc. of ISCSLP*, pages 1–4, December.

Y.-J. Wu, Y. Nankaku, and K. Tokuda. 2009. State mapping based method for cross-lingual speaker adaptation in HMM-based speech synthesis. In *Proc. of Interspeech*, pages 528–531, September.

J. Yamagishi, T. Nose, H. Zen, Z.-H. Ling, T. Toda, K. Tokuda, S. King, and S. Renals. 2009. Robust speaker-adaptive HMM-based text-to-speech synthesis. *IEEE Trans. Audio, Speech and Language Process.*, 17(6):1208–1230. (in press).

J. Yamagishi, B. Usabaev, S. King, O. Watts, J. Dines, J. Tian, R. Hu, K. Oura, K. Tokuda, R. Karhila, and M. Kurimo. 2010. Thousands of voices for hmm-based speech synthesis. *IEEE Trans. Speech, Audio & Language Process.* (in press).

S. Young, G. Everman, D. Kershaw, G. Moore, J. Odell, D. Ollason, V. Valtchev, and P. Woodland, 2001. *The HTK Book Version 3.1*, December.

Hunting for the Black Swan: Risk Mining from Text

Jochen L. Leidner and **Frank Schilder**
Thomson Reuters Corporation
Research & Development
610 Opperman Drive, St. Paul, MN 55123 USA
FirstName.LastName@ThomsonReuters.com

Abstract

In the business world, analyzing and dealing with risk permeates all decisions and actions. However, to date, *risk identification*, the first step in the risk management cycle, has always been a manual activity with little to no intelligent software tool support. In addition, although companies are required to list risks to their business in their annual SEC filings in the USA, these descriptions are often very high-level and vague.

In this paper, we introduce *Risk Mining*, which is the task of identifying a set of risks pertaining to a business area or entity. We argue that by combining Web mining and Information Extraction (IE) techniques, risks can be detected automatically before they materialize, thus providing valuable business intelligence.

We describe a system that induces a risk taxonomy with concrete risks (e.g., interest rate changes) at its leaves and more abstract risks (e.g., financial risks) closer to its root node. The taxonomy is induced via a bootstrapping algorithms starting with a few seeds. The risk taxonomy is used by the system as input to a risk monitor that matches risk mentions in financial documents to the abstract risk types, thus bridging a lexical gap. Our system is able to automatically generate company specific "risk maps", which we demonstrate for a corpus of earnings report conference calls.

1 Introduction

Any given human activity with a particular intended outcome is bound to face a non-zero likelihood of failure. In business, companies are exposed to market risks such as new competitors, disruptive technologies, change in customer attitudes, or a changes in government legislation that can dramatically affect their profitability or threaten their business model or mode of operation. Therefore, any tool to assist in the elicitation of otherwise unforeseen risk factors carries tremendous potential value.

However, it is very hard to identify risks exhaustively, and some types (commonly referred to as the *unknown unknowns*) are especially elusive: if a *known unknown* is the established knowledge that important risk factors are known, but it is unclear whether and when they become realized, then an *unknown unknown* is the lack of awareness, in practice or in principle, of circumstances that may impact the outcome of a project, for example. Nassim Nicholas Taleb calls these "black swans" (Taleb, 2007).

Companies in the US are required to disclose a list of potential risks in their annual Form 10-K SEC fillings in order to warn (potential) investors, and risks are frequently the topic of conference phone calls about a company's earnings. These risks are often reported in general terms, in particular, because it is quite difficult to pinpoint the *unknown unknown*, i.e. what kind of risk is concretely going to materialize. On the other hand, there is a stream of valuable evidence available on the Web, such as news messages, blog entries, and analysts' reports talking about companies' performance and products. Financial analysts and risk officers in large companies have not enjoyed any text analytics support so far, and risk lists devised using questionnaires or interviews are unlikely to be exhaustive due to small sample size, a gap which we aim to address in this paper.

To this end, we propose to use a combination of Web Mining (WM) and Information Eextraction (IE) to assist humans interested in risk (with respect to an organization) and to bridge the gap between the general language and concrete risks. We describe our system, which is divided in two main parts: (a) an offline **Risk Miner** that facilitates the *risk identification* step of the risk management process, and an online (b) **Risk Monitor** that supports the *risk monitoring* step (cf. Figure 2). In addition, a **Risk Mapper** can aggregate and visualize the evidence in the form of a *risk map*. Our risk mining algorithm combines Riloff hyponym patterns with recursive Web pattern bootstrapping and a graph representation.

We do not know of any other implemented end-to-end system for computer-assisted risk identification/visualization using text mining technology.

Proceedings of the ACL 2010 System Demonstrations, pages 54–59,
Uppsala, Sweden, 13 July 2010. ©2010 Association for Computational Linguistics

2 Related Work

Financial IE. IE systems have been applied to the financial domain on Message Understanding Contest (MUC) like tasks, ranging from named entity tagging to slot filling in templates (Costantino, 1992).

Automatic Knowledge Acquisition. (Hearst, 1992) pioneered the pattern-based extraction of hyponyms from corpora, which laid the groundwork for subsequent work, and which included extraction of knowledge from to the Web (e.g. (Etzioni et al., 2004)). To improve precision was the mission of (Kozareva et al., 2008), which was designed to extract hyponymy, but they did so at the expense of recall, using longer *dual anchored patterns* and a pattern linkage graph. However, their method is by its very nature unable to deal with low-frequency items, and their system does not contain a chunker, so only single term items can be extracted. De Saenger et al. (De Saeger et al., 2008) describe an approach that extracts instances of the "trouble" or "obstacle" relations from the Web in the form of pairs of fillers for these binary relations. Their approach, which is described for the Japanese language, uses support vector machine learning and relies on a Japanese syntactic parser, which permits them to process negation. In contrast, and unlike their method, we pursue a more general, open-ended search process, which does not impose as much a priori knowledge. Also, they create a set of pairs, whereas our approach creates a taxonomy tree as output. Most importantly though, our approach is not driven by frequency, and was instead designed to work especially with rare occurrences in mind to permit "black swan"-type risk discovery.

Correlation of Volatility and Text. (Kogan et al., 2009) study the correlation between share price volatility, a proxy for risk, and a set of trigger words occurring in 60,000 SEC 10-K filings from 1995-2006. Since the disclosure of a company's risks is mandatory by law, SEC reports provide a rich source. Their trigger words are selected a priori by humans; in contrast, risk mining as exercised in this paper aims to find risk-indicative words and phrases automatically.

Kogan and colleagues attempt to find a regression model using very simple unigram features based on whole documents that predicts volatility, whereas our goal is to automatically extract patterns to be used as alerts.

Speculative Language & NLP. Light et al. (Light et al., 2004) found that sub-string matching of 14 pre-defined string literals outperforms an SVM classifier using bag-of-words features in the task of speculative language detection in medical abstracts. (Goldberg et al., 2009) are concerned with automatic recognition of human wishes, as expressed in human notes for Year's Eve. They use a bi-partite graph-based approach, where one kind of node (content node) represents things people wish for ("`world peace`") and the other kind of node (template nodes) represent templates that extract them (e.g. "`I wish for` ____"). Wishes can be seen as positive Q, in our formalization.

3 Data

We apply the mined risk extraction patterns to a corpus of financial documents. The data originates from the StreetEvents database and was kindly provided to us by Starmine, a Thomson Reuters company. In particular, we are dealing with 170k earning calls transcripts, a text type that contains monologue (company executives reporting about their company's performance and general situation) as well as dialogue (in the form of questions and answers at the end of each conference call). Participants typically include select business analysts from investment banks, and the calls are published afterwards for the shareholders' benefits. Figure 1 shows some example excerpts. We randomly took a sample of N=6,185 transcripts to use them in our risk alerting experiments.[1]

4 Method

4.1 System

The overall system is divided into two core parts: (a) Risk Mining and (b) Risk Monitoring (cf. Figure 2). For demonstration purposes, we add a (c) Risk Mapper, a visualization component. We describe how a variety of risks can be identified given a normally very high-level description of risks, as one can find in earnings reports, other financial news, or the risk section of 10-K SEC filings. Starting with rather abstract descriptions such as *operational risks* and hyponym-inducing pattern "`< RISK > such as *`", we use the Web to mine pages from which we can harvest additional,

[1] We could also use this data for risk mining, but did not try this due to the small size of the dataset compared to the Web.

CEO: As announced last evening, during our third quarter, we will take the difficult but necessary step to seize [cease] manufacturing at our nearly 100 year old Pennsylvania House casegood plant in Lewisburg, Pennsylvania as well as the nearby Pennsylvania House dining room chair assembly facility in White Deer. Also, the three Lewisburg area warehouses will be consolidated as we assess the logistical needs of the casegood group's existing warehouse operations at an appropriate time in the future to minimize any disruption of service to our customers. This will result in the loss of 425 jobs or approximately 15% of the casegood group's current employee base.

Analyst: Okay, so your comments – and I guess I don't know – I can figure out, as you correctly helped me through, what dollar contribution at GE. I don't know the net equipment sales number last quarter and this quarter. But it sounded like from your comments that if you exclude these fees, that equipment sales were probably flattish. Is that fair to say?
CEO: We're not breaking out the origination fee from the equipment fee, but I think in total, I would say flattish to slightly up.

Figure 1: Example sentences from the earnings conference call dataset. Top: main part. Bottom: Q&A.

and eventually more concrete, candidates, and relate them to risk types via a transitive chain of binary IS-A relations. Contrary to the related work, we use a base NP chunker and download the full pages returned by the search engine rather than search snippets in order to be able to extract risk phrases rather than just terms, which reduces contextual ambiguity and thus increases overall precision. The taxonomy learning method described in the following subsection determines a risk taxonomy and new risks patterns.

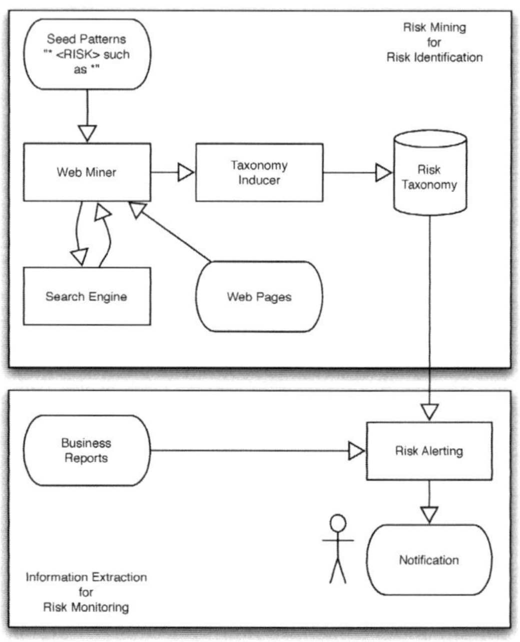

Figure 2: The risk mining and monitoring system architecture

The second part of the system, the Risk Monitor, takes the risks from the risk taxonomy and uses them for monitoring financial text streams such as news, SEC filings, or (in our use case) earnings reports. Using this, an analyst is then able to identify concrete risks in news messages and link them to the high-level risk descriptions. He or she may want to identify operational risks such as fraud for a particular company, for instance. The risk taxonomy can also derive further risks in this category (e.g., faulty components, brakes) for exploration and drill-down analysis. Thus, news reports about faulty breaks in (e.g. Toyota) or volcano outbreaks (e.g. Iceland) can be directly linked to the risk as stated in earnings reports or security filings.

Our Risk Miner and Risk Monitor are implemented in Perl, with the graph processing of the taxonomy implemented in SWI-Prolog, whereas the Risk Mapper exists in two versions, a static image generator for R[2] and, alternatively, an interactive Web page (DHTML, JavaScript, and using Google's Chart API). We use the Yahoo Web search API.

4.2 Taxonomy induction method

Using frequency to compute confidence in a pattern does not work for risk mining, however, because mention of particular risks might be rare. Instead of frequency based indicators (n-grams, frequency weights), we rely on two types of structural confidence validation, namely (a) previously identified risks and (b) previously acquired structural patterns. Note, however, that we can still use PageRank, a popularity-based graph algorithm, because multiple patterns might be connected to a risk term or phrase, even in the absence of frequency counts for each (i.e., we interpret popularity as having multiple sources of support).

1. Risk Candidate Extraction Step. The first step is used to extract a list of risks based on high precision patterns. However, it has been shown that the use of such patterns (e.g., *such as*) quickly lead to an decrease in precision. Ideally, we want to retrieve specific risks by re-applying the the extract risk descriptions:

[2]`http://www.r-project.org`

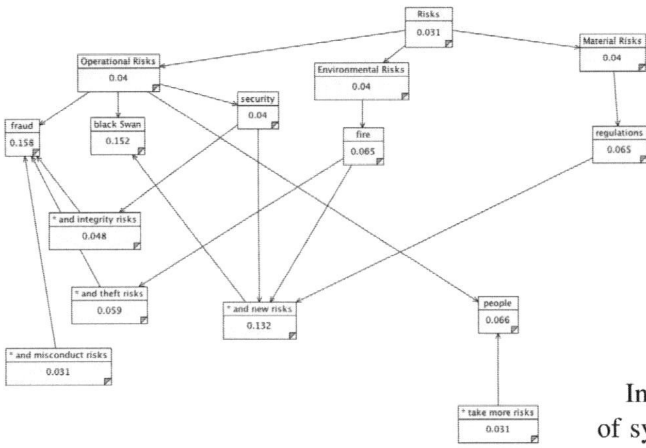

Figure 3: A sample IS-A and Pattern network with sample PageRank scores.

(a) Take a seed, instantiate "< SEED > `such as *`" pattern with seed, extract candidates:

Input: risks

Method: apply pattern "< SEED > `such as` < INSTANCE > ", where < SEED > = risks

Output: list of instances (e.g., *faulty components*)

(b) For each candidate from the list of instances, we find a set of additional candidate hyponyms.

Input: faulty components

Method: apply pattern "< SEED > `such as` < INSTANCE > ", where < SEED > = faulty components

Output: list of instances (e.g., *brake*)

2. Risk Validation. Since the Risk Candidate extraction step will also find many false positives, we need to factor in information that validates that the extracted risk is indeed a risk. We do this by constructing a possible pattern containing this new risk.

(a) Append "`* risks`" to the output of 1(b) in order to make sure that the candidate occurs in a risk context.

Input: brake(s)

Pattern: "`brake(s) * risk(s)`"

Output: a list of patterns (e.g., *minimize such risks*, *raising the risk*)

(b) extract new risk pattern by substituting the risk candidate with < RISK > ; creating a limited number of variations

Input: list of all patterns mined from step 2 (a)

Method: create more pattern variations, such as "< RISK > `minimize such risks`", "`raising the risk of` < RISK > " etc.

Output: list of new potential risks (e.g., *deflation*), but also many false positives (e.g., *way*, as in *The best way to minimize such risks*).

In order to benefit from any human observations of system errors in future runs, we also extended the system so as to read in a partial list of predefined risks at startup time, which can guide the risk miner; while technically different from active learning, this approach was somewhat inspired by it (but our feedback is more loose).

3. Constructing Risk Graph. We have now reached the point where we constructed a graph with risks and patterns. Risks are connected via IS-A links; risks and patterns are connected via PATTERN links. Note that there are links from risks to patterns and from patterns to risks; some risks back-pointed by a pattern may actually not be a risk (e.g., *people*). However, this node is also not connected to a more abstract risk node and will therefore have a low PageRank score. Risks that are connected to patterns that have a high authority (i.e., pointing to by many other links) are highly ranked within PageRank (Figure 3). The risk *black Swan*, for example, has only one pattern it occurs in, but this pattern can be filled by many other risks (e.g., fire, regulations). Hence, the PageRank score of the black swan is high similar to well known risks, such as *fraud*.

4.3 Risk alerting method

We compile the risk taxonomy into a trie automaton, and create a second trie for company names from the meta-data of our corpus. The Risk Monitor reads the two tries and uses the first to detect mentions of risks in the earning reports and the second one to tag company names, both using case-insensitive matching for better recall. Optionally, we can use Porter stemming during trie construction and matching to trade precision for even higher recall, but in the experiments reported here this is not used. Once a signal term or phrase matches, we look up its risk type in a hash table, take a note of the company that the current earnings report is about, and increase the frequency

```
liquidity IS-A financial risks
credit IS-A financial risks
direct risks IS-A financial risks
fraud IS-A financial risks
irregular activity IS-A operational risks
process failure IS-A operational risks
human error IS-A operational risks
labor strikes IS-A operational risks
customer acceptance IS-A IT market risks
interest rate changes IS-A capital market risks
uncertainty IS-A market risks
volatility IS-A mean reverting market risks
copyright infringement IS-A legal risks
negligence IS-A other legal risks
an unfair dismissal IS-A the legal risks
Sarbanes IS-A legal risks
government changes IS-A global political risks
crime IS-A Social and political risks
state intervention IS-A political risks
terrorist acts IS-A geopolitical risks
earthquakes IS-A natural disaster risks
floods IS-A natural disaster risks
global climate change IS-A environmental risks
severe and extreme weather IS-A environmental risks
internal cracking IS-A any technological risks
GM technologies IS-A tech risks
scalability issues IS-A technology risks
viruses IS-A the technical risks
```

Figure 4: Selected financial risk tuples after Web validation.

count for this ⟨company; risk type⟩ tuple, which we use for graphic rendering purposes.

4.4 Risk mapping method

To demonstrate the method presented here, we created a visualization that displays a *risk map*, which is a two dimensional table showing companies and the types of risk they are facing, together with bubble sizes proportional to the number of alerts that the Risk Monitor could discover in the corpus. The second option also permits the user to explore the detected risk mentions per company and by risk type.

5 Results

From the Web mining process, we obtain a set of pairs (Figure 4), from which the taxonomy is constructed. In one run with only 12 seeds (just the risk type names with variants), we obtained a taxonomy with 280 validated leave nodes that are connected transitively to the risks root node.

Our resulting system produces visualizations we call "risk maps", because they graphically present the extracted risk types in aggregated form. A set of risk types can be selected for presentation as well as a set of companies of interest. A risk map display is then generated using either R (Figure 5) or an interactive Web page, depending on the user's preference.

Qualitative error analysis. We inspected the output of the risk miner and observed the following classes of issues: (a) chunker errors: if phrasal boundaries are placed at the wrong position, the taxonomy will include wrong relations. For example, deictic determiners such as "this" were a problem (e.g. `that IS-A indirect risks`) before we introduced a stop word filter that discards candidate tuples that contain no content words. Another prominent example is "short term" instead of the correct "short term risk"; (b) *semantic drift*[3]: due to polysemy, words and phrases can denote risk and non-risk meanings, depending on context. Talking about risks even a specific pattern such as "such as" [sic] is used by authors to induce a variety of perspectives on the topic of risk, and after several iterations negative effects of type (a) errors compound; (c) off-topic relations: the seeds are designed to induce a taxonomy specific to risk types. As a side effect, many (correct or incorrect) irrelevant relations are learned, e.g. `credit and debit cards is-a money transfer`. We currently discard these by virtue of ignoring all relations not transitively connected with the root node `risks`, so no formalized domain knowledge is required; (d) overlap: the concept space is divided up differently by different writers, both on the Web and in the risk management literature, and this is reflected by multiple category membership of many risks (e.g. is cash flow primarily an operational risk or a financial risk?). Currently, we do not deal with this phenomenon automatically; (e) redundant relations: at the time of writing, we do not cache all already extracted and validated risks/non-risks. This means there is room for improvement w.r.t. runtime, because we make more Web queries than strictly necessary. While we have not evaluated this system yet, we found by in-

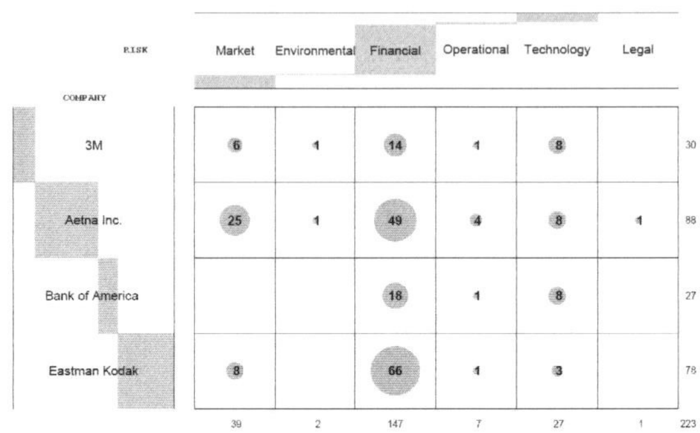

Figure 5: An Example Risk Map.

[3]to use a term coined by Andy Lauriston

specting the output that our method is particularly effective for learning natural disasters and medical conditions, probably because they are well-covered by news sites and biomedical abstracts on the Web. We also found that some classes contain more noise than others, for example operational risk was less precise than financial risk, probably due to the lesser specificity of the former risk type.

6 Summary, Conclusions & Future Work

Summary of Contributions.

In this paper, we introduced the task of risk mining, which produces patterns that are useful in another task, risk alerting. Both tasks provide computational assistance to risk-related decision making in the financial sector. We described a special-purpose algorithm for inducing a risk taxonomy offline, which can then be used online to analyze earning reports in order to signal risks. In doing so, we have addressed two research questions of general relevance, namely how to extract *rare patterns*, for which frequency-based methods fail, and how to use the Web to bridge the *vocabulary gap*, i.e. how to match up terms and phrases in financial news prose with the more abstract language typically used in talking about risk in general.

We have described an implemented demonstrator system comprising an offline risk taxonomy miner, an online risk alerter and a visualization component that creates visual risk maps by company and risk type, which we have applied to a corpus of earnings call transcripts.

Future Work. Extracted negative and also positive risks can be used in many applications, ranging from *e-mail alerts* to determinating *credit ratings*. Our preliminary work on risk maps can be put on a more theoretical footing (Hunter, 2000). After studying further how output of risk alerting correlates[4] with non-textual signals like share price, risk detection signals could inform human or trading decisions.

Acknowledgments. We are grateful to Khalid Al-Kofahi, Peter Jackson and James Powell for supporting this work. Thanks to George Bonne, Ryan Roser, and Craig D'Alessio at Starmine, a Thomson Reuters company, for sharing the StreetEvents dataset with us, and to David Rosenblatt for discussions and to Jack Conrad for feedback on this paper.

[4]Our hypothesis is that risk patterns can outperform bag of words (Kogan et al., 2009).

References

Marco Costantino. 1992. Financial information extraction using pre-defined and user-definable templates in the LOLITA system. *Proceedings of the Fifteenth International Conference on Computational Linguistics (COLING 1992), vol. 4*, pages 241–255.

Stijn De Saeger, Kentaro Torisawa, and Jun'ichi Kazama. 2008. Looking for trouble. In *Proceedings of the 22nd International Conference on Computational Linguistics (COLING 2008)*, pages 185–192, Morristown, NJ, USA. Association for Computational Linguistics.

Oren Etzioni, Michael J. Cafarella, Doug Downey, Stanley Kok, Ana-Maria Popescu, Tal Shaked, Stephen Soderland, Daniel S. Weld, and Alexander Yates. 2004. Web-scale information extraction in KnowItAll: preliminary results. In Stuart I. Feldman, Mike Uretsky, Marc Najork, and Craig E. Wills, editors, *Proceedings of the 13th international conference on World Wide Web (WWW 2004), New York, NY, USA, May 17-20, 2004*, pages 100–110. ACM.

Andrew B. Goldberg, Nathanael Fillmore, David Andrzejewski, Zhiting Xu, Bryan Gibson, and Xiaojin Zhu. 2009. May all your wishes come true: A study of wishes and how to recognize them. In *Proceedings of Human Language Technologies: The 2009 Annual Conference of the North American Chapter of the Association for Computational Linguistics*, pages 263–271, Boulder, Colorado, June. Association for Computational Linguistics.

Marti Hearst. 1992. Automatic acquisition of hyponyms from large text corpora. In *Proceedings of the Fourteenth International Conference on Computational Linguistics (COLING 1992)*.

Anthony Hunter. 2000. Ramification analysis using causal mapping. *Data and Knowledge Engineering*, 32:200–227.

Shimon Kogan, Dimitry Levin, Bryan R. Routledge, Jacob S. Sagi, and Noah A. Smith. 2009. Predicting risk from financial reports with regression. In *Proceedings of the Joint International Conference on Human Language Technology and the Annual Meeting of the North American Chapter of the Association for Computational Linguistics (HLT-NAACL)*.

Zornitsa Kozareva, Ellen Riloff, and Eduard Hovy. 2008. Semantic class learning from the web with hyponym pattern linkage graphs. In *Proceedings of ACL-HLT*, pages 1048–1056, Columbus, OH, USA. Association for Computational Linguistics.

Marc Light, Xin Ying Qiu, and Padmini Srinivasan. 2004. The language of bioscience: Facts, speculations, and statements in between. In *BioLINK 2004: Linking Biological Literature, Ontologies and Databases*, pages 17–24. ACL.

Nassim Nicholas Taleb. 2007. *The Black Swan: The Impact of the Highly Improbable*. Random House.

Speech-driven Access to the Deep Web on Mobile Devices

Taniya Mishra and **Srinivas Bangalore**
AT&T Labs - Research
180 Park Avenue
Florham Park, NJ 07932 USA.
{taniya,srini}@research.att.com.

Abstract

The Deep Web is the collection of information repositories that are not indexed by search engines. These repositories are typically accessible through web forms and contain dynamically changing information. In this paper, we present a system that allows users to access such rich repositories of information on mobile devices using spoken language.

1 Introduction

The World Wide Web (WWW) is the largest repository of information known to mankind. It is generally agreed that the WWW continues to significantly enrich and transform our lives in unprecedent ways. Be that as it may, the WWW that we encounter is limited by the information that is accessible through search engines. Search engines, however, do not index a large portion of WWW that is variously termed as the *Deep Web*, *Hidden Web*, or *Invisible Web*.

Deep Web is the information that is in proprietory databases. Information in such databases is usually more structured and changes at higher frequency than textual web pages. It is conjectured that the Deep Web is 500 times the size of the surface web. Search engines are unable to index this information and hence, unable to retrieve it for the user who may be searching for such information. So, the only way for users to access this information is to find the appropriate web-form, fill in the necessary search parameters, and use it to query the database that contains the information that is being searched for. Examples of such web forms include, movie, train and bus times, and airline/hotel/restaurant reservations.

Contemporaneously, the devices to access information have moved out of the office and home environment into the open world. The ubiquity of mobile devices has made information access an any time, any place activity. However, information access using text input on mobile devices is tedious and unnatural because of the limited screen space and the small (or soft) keyboards. In addition, by the *mobile* nature of these devices, users often like to use them in hands-busy environments, ruling out the possibility of typing text. Filling web-forms using the small screens and tiny keyboards of mobile devices is neither easy nor quick.

In this paper, we present a system, `Qme!`, designed towards providing a spoken language interface to the Deep Web. In its current form, `Qme!` provides a unifed interface onn iPhone (shown in Figure 1) that can be used by users to search for *static* and *dynamic* questions. *Static* questions are questions whose answers to these questions remain the same irrespective of when and where the questions are asked. Examples of such questions are *What is the speed of light?*, *When is George Washington's birthday?*. For *static* questions, the system retrieves the answers from an archive of human generated answers to questions. This ensures higher accuracy for the answers retrieved (if found in the archive) and also allows us to retrieve related questions on the user's topic of interest.

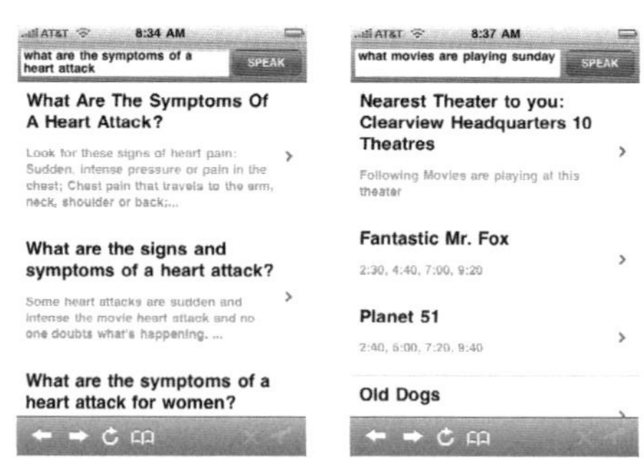

Figure 1: Retrieval results for static and dynamic questions using `Qme!`

Dynamic questions are questions whose answers depend on when and where they are asked. Examples of such questions are *What is the stock price of General Motors?*, *Who won the game last night?*, *What is playing at the theaters near me?*.

Proceedings of the ACL 2010 System Demonstrations, pages 60–65,
Uppsala, Sweden, 13 July 2010. ©2010 Association for Computational Linguistics

The answers to dynamic questions are often part of the Deep Web. Our system retrieves the answers to such dynamic questions by parsing the questions to retrieve pertinent search keywords, which are in turn used to query information databases accessible over the Internet using web forms. However, the internal distinction between dynamic and static questions, and the subsequent differential treatment within the system is seamless to the user. The user simply uses a single unified interface to ask a question and receive a collection of *answers* that potentially address her question directly.

The layout of the paper is as follows. In Section 2, we present the system architecture. In Section 3, we present bootstrap techniques to distinguish dynamic questions from static questions, and evaluate the efficacy of these techniques on a test corpus. In Section 4, we show how our system retrieves answers to dynamic questions. In Section 5, we show how our system retrieves answers to static questions. We conclude in Section 6.

2 Speech-driven Question Answer System

Speech-driven access to information has been a popular application deployed by many companies on a variety of information resources (Microsoft, 2009; Google, 2009; YellowPages, 2009; vlingo.com, 2009). In this prototype demonstration, we describe a speech-driven question-answer application. The system architecture is shown in Figure 2.

The user of this application provides a spoken language query to a mobile device intending to find an answer to the question. The speech recognition module of the system recognizes the spoken query. The result from the speech recognizer can be either a single-best string or a weighted word lattice.[1] This textual output of recognition is then used to classify the user query either as a dynamic query or a static query. If the user query is static, the result of the speech recognizer is used to search a large corpus of question-answer pairs to retrieve the relevant answers. The retrieved results are ranked using $tf.idf$ based metric discussed in Section 5. If the user query is dynamic, the answers are retrieved by querying a web form from the appropriate web site (e.g *www.fandango.com* for movie information). In Figure 1, we illustrate the answers that `Qme!` returns for static and dynamic questions.

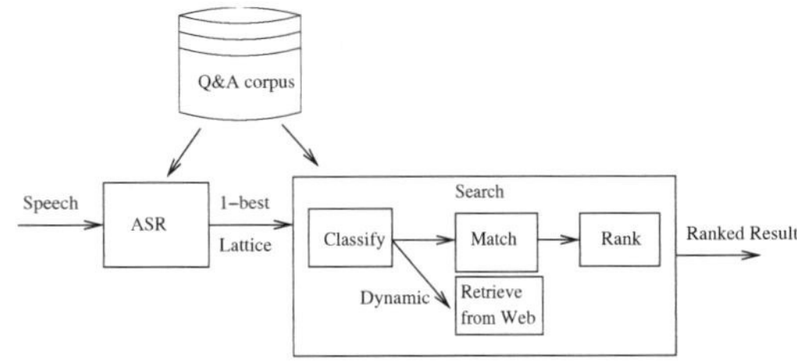

Figure 2: The architecture of the speech-driven question-answering system

2.1 Demonstration

In the demonstration, we plan to show the users static and dynamic query handling on an iPhone using spoken language queries. Users can use the iphone and speak their queries using an interface provided by `Qme!`. A Wi-Fi access spot will make this demonstation more compelling.

3 Dynamic and Static Questions

As mentioned in the introduction, dynamic questions require accessing the hidden web through a web form with the appropriate parameters. Answers to dynamic questions cannot be preindexed as can be done for static questions. They depend on the time and geographical location of the question. In dynamic questions, there may be no explicit reference to time, unlike the questions in the TERQAS corpus (Radev and Sundheim., 2002) which explicitly refer to the temporal properties of the entities being questioned or the relative ordering of past and future events.

The time-dependency of a dynamic question lies in the temporal nature of its answer. For example, consider the question, *What is the address of the theater White Christmas is playing at in New York?*. White Christmas is a seasonal play that plays in New York every year for a few weeks in December and January, but not necessarily at the same theater every year. So, depending when this question is asked, the answer will be different. If the question is asked in the summer, the answer will be "This play is not currently playing anywhere in NYC." If the question is asked during December, 2009, the answer might be different than the answer given in December 2010, because the theater at which White Christmas is playing differs from 2009 to 2010.

There has been a growing interest in temporal analysis for question-answering since the late 1990's. Early work on temporal expressions iden-

[1]For this paper, the ASR used to recognize these utterances incorporates an acoustic model adapted to speech collected from mobile devices and a four-gram language model that is built from the corpus of questions.

tification using a tagger culminated in the development of TimeML (Pustejovsky et al., 2001), a markup language for annotating temporal expressions and events in text. Other examples include, QA-by-Dossier with Constraints (Prager et al., 2004), a method of improving QA accuracy by asking auxiliary questions related to the original question in order to temporally verify and restrict the original answer. (Moldovan et al., 2005) detect and represent temporally related events in natural language using logical form representation. (Saquete et al., 2009) use the temporal relations in a question to decompose it into simpler questions, the answers of which are recomposed to produce the answers to the original question.

3.1 Question Classification: Dynamic and Static Questions

We automatically classify questions as dynamic and static questions. The answers to static questions can be retrieved from the QA archive. To answer dynamic questions, we query the database(s) associated with the topic of the question through web forms on the Internet. We first use a topic classifier to detect the topic of a question followed by a dynamic/static classifier trained on questions related to a topic, as shown in Figure 3. For the question *what movies are playing around me?*, we detect it is a movie related dynamic question and query a movie information web site (e.g. www.fandango.com) to retrieve the results based on the user's GPS information.

Dynamic questions often contain temporal indexicals, i.e., expressions of the form *today, now, this week, two summers ago, currently, recently*, etc. Our initial approach was to use such signal words and phrases to automatically identify dynamic questions. The chosen signals were based on annotations in TimeML. We also included spatial indexicals, such as *here* and other clauses that were observed to be contained in dynamic questions such as *cost of*, and *how much is* in the list of signal phrases. These signals words and phrases were encoded into a regular-expression-based recognizer.

This regular-expression based recognizer identified 3.5% of our dataset – which consisted of several million questions – as dynamic. The type of questions identified were *What is playing in the movie theaters tonight?*, *What is tomorrow's weather forecast for LA?*, *Where can I go to get Thai food near here?* However, random samplings of the same dataset, annotated by four independent human labelers, indicated that on average 13.5% of the dataset is considered dynamic. This shows that the temporal and spatial indexicals encoded as a regular-expression based recognizer is unable to identify a large percentage of the dynamic questions.

This approach leaves out dynamic questions that do not contain temporal or spatial indexicals. For example, *What is playing at AMC Loew's?*, or *What is the score of the Chargers and Dolphines game?*. For such examples, considering the tense of the verb in question may help. The last two examples are both in the present continuous tense. But verb tense does not help for a question such as *Who got voted off Survivor?*. This question is certainly dynamic. The information that is most likely being sought by this question is what is the name of the person who got voted off the TV show Survivor *most recently*, and not what is the name of the person (or persons) who have gotten voted off the Survivor at some point in the past.

Knowing the broad topic (such as movies, current affairs, and music) of the question may be very useful. It is likely that there may be many dynamic questions about movies, sports, and finance, while history and geography may have few or none. This idea is bolstered by the following analysis. The questions in our dataset are annotated with a broad topic tag. Binning the 3.5% of our dataset identified as dynamic questions by their broad topic produced a long-tailed distribution. Of the 104 broad topics, the top-5 topics contained over 50% of the dynamic questions. These top five topics were sports, TV and radio, events, movies, and finance.

Considering the issues laid out in the previous section, our classification approach is to chain two machine-learning-based classifiers: a topic classifier chained to a dynamic/static classifier, as shown in Figure 3. In this architecture, we build one topic classifier, but several dynamic/static classifiers, each trained on data pertaining to one broad topic.

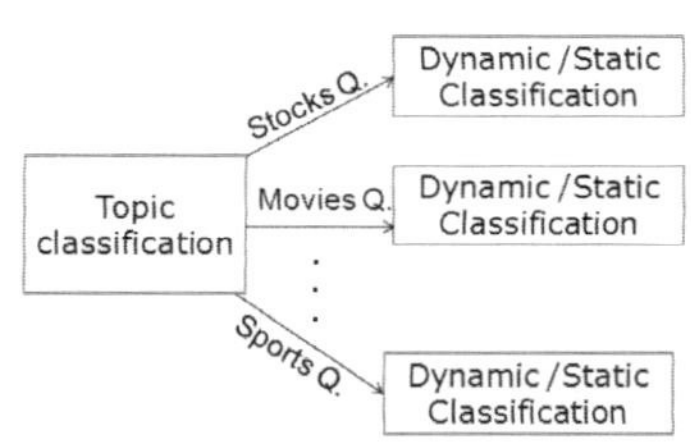

Figure 3: Chaining two classifiers

We used supervised learning to train the topic

classifier, since our entire dataset is annotated by human experts with topic labels. In contrast, to train a dynamic/static classifier, we experimented with the following three different techniques.

Baseline: We treat questions as dynamic if they contain temporal indexicals, e.g. *today*, *now*, *this week*, *two summers ago*, *currently*, *recently*, which were based on the TimeML corpus. We also included spatial indexicals such as *here*, and other substrings such as *cost of* and *how much is*. A question is considered static if it does not contain any such words/phrases.

Self-training with bagging: The general self-training with bagging algorithm (Banko and Brill, 2001). The benefit of self-training is that we can build a better classifier than that built from the small seed corpus by simply adding in the large unlabeled corpus without requiring hand-labeling.

Active-learning: This is another popular method for training classifiers when not much annotated data is available. The key idea in active learning is to annotate only those instances of the dataset that are most difficult for the classifier to learn to classify. It is expected that training classifiers using this method shows better performance than if samples were chosen randomly for the same human annotation effort.

We used the maximum entropy classifier in LLAMA (Haffner, 2006) for all of the above classification tasks. We have chosen the active learning classifier due to its superior performance and integrated it into the `Qme!` system. We provide further details about the learning methods in (Mishra and Bangalore, 2010).

3.2 Experiments and Results

3.2.1 Topic Classification

The topic classifier was trained using a training set consisting of over one million questions downloaded from the web which were manually labeled by human experts as part of answering the questions. The test set consisted of 15,000 randomly selected questions. Word trigrams of the question are used as features for a MaxEnt classifier which outputs a score distribution on all of the 104 possible topic labels. The error rate results for models selecting the top topic and the top two topics according to the score distribution are shown in Table 1. As can be seen these error rates are far lower than the baseline model of selecting the most frequent topic.

Model	Error Rate
Baseline	98.79%
Top topic	23.9%
Top-two topics	12.23%

Table 1: Results of topic classification

3.2.2 Dynamic/static Classification

As mentioned before, we experimented with three different approaches to bootstrapping a dynamic/static question classifier. We evaluated these methods on a 250 question test set drawn from the broad topic of *Movies*. The error rates are summarized in Table 2. We provide further details of this experiment in (Mishra and Bangalore, 2010).

Training approach	Lowest Error rate
Baseline	27.70%
"Supervised" learning	22.09%
Self-training	8.84%
Active-learning	4.02%

Table 2: Best Results of dynamic/static classification

4 Retrieving answers to dynamic questions

Following the classification step outlined in Section 3.1, we know whether a user query is static or dynamic, and the broad category of the question. If the question is dynamic, then our system performs a vertical search based on the broad topic of the question. In our system, so far, we have incorporated vertical searches on three broad topics: Movies, Mass Transit, and Yellow Pages.

For each broad topic, we have identified a few trusted content aggregator websites. For example, for dynamic questions related to Movies-related dynamic user queries, `www.fandango.com` is a trusted content aggregator website. Other such trusted content aggregator websites have been identified for Mass Transit related and for Yellow-pages related dynamic user queries. We have also identified the web-forms that can be used to search these aggregator sites and the search parameters that these web-forms need for searching. So, given a user query, whose broad category has been determined and which has been classified as a dynamic query by the system, the next step is to parse the query to obtain pertinent search parameters.

The search parameters are dependent on the broad category of the question, the trusted content aggregator website(s), the web-forms associated with this category, and of course, the content of the user query. From the search parameters, a search query to the associated web-form is issued to search the related aggregator site. For example, for a movie-related query, *What time is Twilight playing in Madison, New Jersey?*, the pertinent search parameters that are parsed out are *movie-name: Twilight*, *city: Madison*, and *state: New Jersey*, which are used to build a search string that Fandango's web-form can use to search the Fandango site. For a yellow-pages type of query, *Where is the Saigon Kitchen in Austin, Texas?*, the pertinent search parameters that are parsed out are *business-name: Saigon Kitchen*, *city: Austin*, and *state: Texas*, which are used to construct a search string to search the Yellowpages website. These are just two examples of the kinds of dynamic user queries that we encounter. Within each broad category, there is a wide variety of the sub-types of user queries, and for each sub-type, we have to parse out different search parameters and use different web-forms. Details of this extraction are presented in (Feng and Bangalore, 2009).

It is quite likely that many of the dynamic queries may not have all the pertinent search parameters explicitly outlined. For example, a mass transit query may be *When is the next train to Princeton?*. The bare minimum search parameters needed to answer this query are a *from-location*, and a *to-location*. However, the *from-location* is not explicitly present in this query. In this case, the *from-location* is inferred using the GPS sensor present on the iPhone (on which our system is built to run). Depending on the web-form that we are querying, it is possible that we may be able to simply use the latitude-longitude obtained from the GPS sensor as the value for the *from-location* parameter. At other times, we may have to perform an intermediate latitude-longitude to city/state (or zip-code) conversion in order to obtain the appropriate search parameter value.

Other examples of dynamic queries in which search parameters are not explicit in the query, and hence, have to be deduced by the system, include queries such as *Where is XMen playing?* and *How long is Ace Hardware open?*. In each of these examples, the user has not specified a location. Based on our understanding of natural language, in such a scenario, our system is built to assume that the user wants to find a movie theatre (or, is referring to a hardware store) *near* where he is currently located. So, the system obtains the user's location from the GPS sensor and uses it to search for a theatre (or locate the hardware store) within a five-mile radius of her location.

In the last few paragraphs, we have discussed how we search for answers to dynamic user queries from the hidden web by using web-forms. However, the search results returned by these web-forms usually cannot be displayed as is in our `Qme!` interface. The reason is that the results are often HTML pages that are designed to be displayed on a desktop or a laptop screen, not a small mobile phone screen. Displaying the results as they are returned from search would make readability difficult. So, we parse the HTML-encoded result pages to get just the answers to the user query and reformat it, to fit the `Qme!` interface, which is designed to be easily readable on the iPhone (as seen in Figure 1).[2]

5 Retrieving answers to static questions

Answers to static user queries – questions whose answers do not change over time – are retrieved in a different way than answers to dynamic questions. A description of how our system retrieves the answers to static questions is presented in this section.

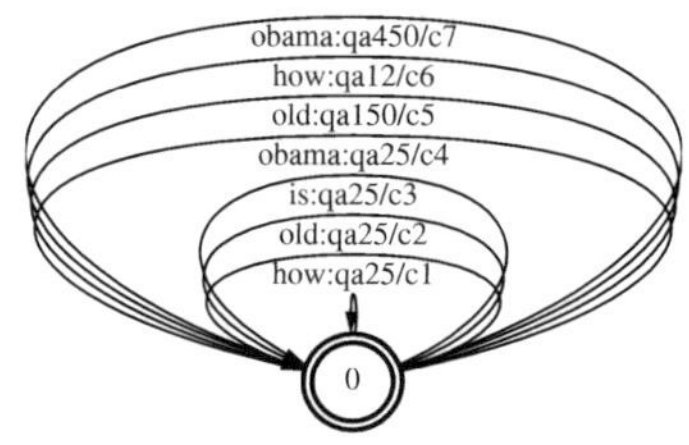

Figure 4: An example of an FST representing the search index.

5.1 Representing Search Index as an FST

To obtain results for static user queries, we have implemented our own search engine using finite-state transducers (FST), in contrast to using Lucene (Hatcher and Gospodnetic., 2004) as it is a more efficient representation of the search index that allows us to consider word lattices output by ASR as input queries.

The FST search index is built as follows. We index each question-answer (QA) pair from our repository ((q_i, a_i), qa_i for short) using the words (w_{q_i}) in question q_i. This index is represented as a weighted finite-state transducer (*SearchFST*) as shown in Figure 4. Here a word w_{q_i} (e.g *old*) is the input symbol for a set of arcs whose output symbol is the index of the QA pairs where *old* appears

[2] We are aware that we could use SOAP (Simple Object Access Protocol) encoding to do the search, however not all aggregator sites use SOAP yet.

in the question. The weight of the arc $c_{(w_{q_i}, q_i)}$ is one of the similarity based weights discussed in Section 4.1. As can be seen from Figure 4, the words *how*, *old*, *is* and *obama* contribute a score to the question-answer pair *qa25*; while other pairs, *qa150, qa12, qa450* are scored by only one of these words.

5.2 Search Process using FSTs

A user's speech query, after speech recognition, is represented as a finite state automaton (FSA, either 1-best or WCN), *QueryFSA*. The *QueryFSA* is then transformed into another FSA (*NgramFSA*) that represents the set of n-grams of the *QueryFSA*. In contrast to most text search engines, where stop words are removed from the query, we weight the query terms with their *idf* values which results in a weighted *NgramFSA*. The *NgramFSA* is composed with the *SearchFST* and we obtain all the arcs $(w_q, qa_{w_q}, c_{(w_q, qa_{w_q})})$ where w_q is a query term, qa_{w_q} is a QA index with the query term and, $c_{(w_q, qa_{w_q})}$ is the weight associated with that pair. Using this information, we aggregate the weight for a QA pair (qa_q) across all query words and rank the retrieved QAs in the descending order of this aggregated weight. We select the top N QA pairs from this ranked list. The query composition, QA weight aggregation and selection of top N QA pairs are computed with finite-state transducer operations as shown in Equations 1 and 2[3]. An evaluation of this search methodology on word lattices is presented in (Mishra and Bangalore, 2010).

$$D = \pi_2(NgramFSA \circ SearchFST) \quad (1)$$

$$TopN = fsmbestpath(fsmdeterminize(D), N) \quad (2)$$

6 Summary

In this demonstration paper, we have presented `Qme!`, a speech-driven question answering system for use on mobile devices. The novelty of this system is that it provides users with a single unified interface for searching both the visible and the hidden web using the most natural input modality for use on mobile phones – spoken language.

7 Acknowledgments

We would like to thank Junlan Feng, Michael Johnston and Mazin Gilbert for the help we received in putting this system together. We would also like to thank ChaCha for providing us the data included in this system.

[3] We have dropped the need to convert the weights into the *real* semiring for aggregation, to simplify the discussion.

References

M. Banko and E. Brill. 2001. Scaling to very very large corpora for natural language disambiguation. In *Proceedings of the 39th annual meeting of the association for computational linguistics: ACL 2001*, pages 26–33.

J. Feng and S. Bangalore. 2009. Effects of word confusion networks on voice search. In *Proceedings of EACL-2009*, Athens, Greece.

Google, 2009. *http://www.google.com/mobile*.

P. Haffner. 2006. Scaling large margin classifiers for spoken language understanding. *Speech Communication*, 48(iv):239–261.

E. Hatcher and O. Gospodnetic. 2004. *Lucene in Action (In Action series)*. Manning Publications Co., Greenwich, CT, USA.

Microsoft, 2009. *http://www.live.com*.

T. Mishra and S. Bangalore. 2010. Qme!: A speech-based question-answering system on mobile devices. In *Proceedings of NAACL-HLT*.

D. Moldovan, C. Clark, and S. Harabagiu. 2005. Temporal context representation and reasoning. In *Proceedings of the 19th International Joint Conference on Artificial Intelligence*, pages 1009–1104.

J. Prager, J. Chu-Carroll, and K. Czuba. 2004. Question answering using constraint satisfaction: Qa-by-dossier-with-contraints. In *Proceedings of the 42nd annual meeting of the association for computational linguistics: ACL 2004*, pages 574–581.

J. Pustejovsky, R. Ingria, R. Saurí, J. Casta no, J. Littman, and R. Gaizauskas., 2001. *The language of time: A reader*, chapter The specification languae – TimeML. Oxford University Press.

D. Radev and B. Sundheim. 2002. Using timeml in question answering. Technical report, Brandies University.

E. Saquete, J. L. Vicedo, P. Martínez-Barco, R. Mu noz, and H. Llorens. 2009. Enhancing qa systems with complex temporal question processing capabilities. *Journal of Artificial Intelligence Research*, 35:775–811.

vlingo.com, 2009. *http://www.vlingomobile.com/downloads.html*.

YellowPages, 2009. *http://www.speak4it.com*.

Tools for Multilingual Grammar-Based Translation on the Web

Aarne Ranta and **Krasimir Angelov** and **Thomas Hallgren**
Department of Computer Science and Engineering
Chalmers University of Technology and University of Gothenburg
aarne@chalmers.se, krasimir@chalmers.se, hallgren@chalmers.se

Abstract

This is a system demo for a set of tools for translating texts between multiple languages in real time with high quality. The translation works on restricted languages, and is based on semantic interlinguas. The underlying model is GF (Grammatical Framework), which is an open-source toolkit for multilingual grammar implementations. The demo will cover up to 20 parallel languages.

Two related sets of tools are presented: grammarian's tools helping to build translators for new domains and languages, and translator's tools helping to translate documents. The grammarian's tools are designed to make it easy to port the technique to new applications. The translator's tools are essential in the restricted language context, enabling the author to remain in the fragments recognized by the system.

The tools that are demonstrated will be applied and developed further in the European project MOLTO (Multilingual On-Line Translation) which has started in March 2010 and runs for three years.

1 Translation Needs for the Web

The best-known translation tools on the web are Google translate[1] and Systran[2]. They are targeted to **consumers** of web documents: users who want to find out what a given document is about. For this purpose, **browsing quality** is sufficient, since the user has intelligence and good will, and understands that she uses the translation at her own risk.

Since Google and Systran translations can be grammatically and semantically flawed, they don't reach **publication quality**, and cannot hence be used by the **producers** of web documents. For instance, the provider of an e-commerce site cannot take the risk that the product descriptions or selling conditions have errors that change the original intentions.

There are very few automatic translation systems actually in use for producers of information. As already noted by Bar-Hillel (1964), machine translation is one of those AI-complete tasks that involves a trade-off between coverage and precision, and the current mainstream systems opt for coverage. This is also what web users expect: they want to be able to throw just anything at the translation system and get something useful back. Precision-oriented approaches, the prime example of which is METEO (Chandioux 1977), have not been popular in recent years.

However, from the producer's point of view, large coverage is not essential: unlike the consumer's tools, their input is predictable, and can be restricted to very specific domains, and to content that the producers themselves are creating in the first place. But even in such tasks, two severe problems remain:

- The **development cost problem**: a large amount of work is needed for building translators for new domains and new languages.

- The **authoring problem**: since the method does not work for all input, the author of the source text of translation may need special training to write in a way that can be translated at all.

These two problems have probably been the main obstacles to making high-quality restricted language translation more wide-spread in tasks where it would otherwise be applicable. We address these problems by providing tools that help developers of translation systems on the one hand, and authors and translators—i.e. the users of the systems—on the other.

In the MOLTO project (Multilingual On-Line Translation)[3], we have the goal to improve both the development and use of restricted language translation by an order of magnitude, as compared with the state of the art. As for development costs, this means that a system for many languages and with adequate quality can be built in a matter of days rather than months. As for authoring, this means that content production does not require the use of manuals or involve trial and error, both of which can easily make the work ten times slower than normal writing.

In the proposed system demo, we will show how some of the building blocks for MOLTO can already now be used in web-based translators, although on a

[1] www.google.com/translate

[2] www.systransoft.com

[3] www.molto-project.eu

Proceedings of the ACL 2010 System Demonstrations, pages 66–71,
Uppsala, Sweden, 13 July 2010. ©2010 Association for Computational Linguistics

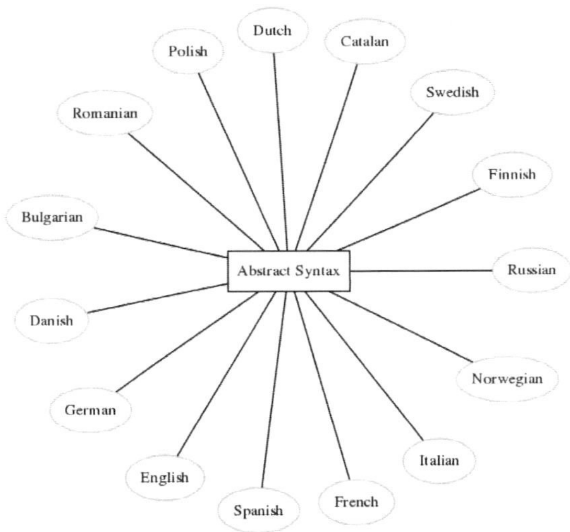

Figure 1: A multilingual GF grammar with reversible mappings from a common abstract syntax to the 15 languages currently available in the GF Resource Grammar Library.

smaller scale as regards languages and application domains. A running demo system is available at `http://grammaticalframework.org:41296`.

2 Multilingual Grammars

The translation tools are based on **GF**, **Grammatical Framework**[4] (Ranta 2004). GF is a **grammar formalism**—that is, a mathematical model of natural language, equipped with a formal notation for writing grammars and a computer program implementing parsing and generation which are declaratively defined by grammars. Thus GF is comparable with formalism such as HPSG (Pollard and Sag 1994), LFG (Bresnan 1982) or TAG (Joshi 1985). The novel feature of GF is the notion of **multilingual grammars**, which describe several languages simultaneously by using a common representation called **abstract syntax**; see Figure 1.

In a multilingual GF grammar, meaning-preserving translation is provided as a composition of parsing and generation via the abstract syntax, which works as an **interlingua**. This model of translation is different from approaches based on other comparable grammar formalisms, such as synchronous TAGs (Shieber and Schabes 1990), Pargram (Butt & al. 2002, based on LFG), LINGO Matrix (Bender and Flickinger 2005, based on HPSG), and CLE (Core Language Engine, Alshawi 1992). These approaches use **transfer rules** between individual languages, separate for each pair of languages.

Being interlingua-based, GF translation scales up linearly to new languages without the quadratic blow-up of transfer-based systems. In transfer-based systems, as many as $n(n-1)$ components (transfer functions) are needed to cover all language pairs in both directions. In an interlingua-based system, $2n+1$ components are enough: the interlingua itself, plus translations in both directions between each language and the interlingua. However, in GF, $n+1$ components are sufficient, because the mappings from the abstract syntax to each language (the **concrete syntaxes**) are **reversible**, i.e. usable for both generation and parsing.

Multilingual GF grammars can be seen as an implementation of Curry's distinction between **tectogrammatical** and **phenogrammatical** structure (Curry 1961). In GF, the tectogrammatical structure is called abstract syntax, following standard computer science terminology. It is defined by using a **logical framework** (Harper & al. 1993), whose mathematical basis is in the **type theory** of Martin-Löf (1984). Two things can be noted about this architecture, both showing improvements over state-of-the-art grammar-based translation methods.

First, the translation interlingua (the abstract syntax) is a powerful logical formalism, able to express semantical structures such as context-dependencies and anaphora (Ranta 1994). In particular, dependent types make it more expressive than the type theory used in Montague grammar (Montague 1974) and employed in the Rosetta translation project (Rosetta 1998).

Second, GF uses a **framework for interlinguas**, rather than one universal interlingua. This makes the interlingual approach more light-weight and feasible than in systems assuming one universal interlingua, such as Rosetta and UNL, Universal Networking Language[5]. It also gives more precision to special-purpose translation: the interlingua of a GF translation system (i.e. the abstract syntax of a multilingual grammar) can encode precisely those structures and distinctions that are relevant for the task at hand. Thus an interlingua for mathematical proofs (Hallgren and Ranta 2000) is different from one for commands for operating an MP3 player (Perera and Ranta 2007). The expressive power of the logical framework is sufficient for both kinds of tasks.

One important source of inspiration for GF was the WYSIWYM system (Power and Scott 1998), which used domain-specific interlinguas and produced excellent quality in multilingual generation. But the generation components were hard-coded in the program, instead of being defined declaratively as in GF, and they were not usable in the direction of parsing.

3 Grammars and Ontologies

Parallel to the first development efforts of GF in the late 1990's, another framework idea was emerging in web technology: XML, Extensible Mark-up Language, which unlike HTML is not a single mark-up language but a framework for creating custom mark-up lan-

[4] `www.grammaticalframework.org`

[5] `www.undl.org`

guages. The analogy between GF and XML was seen from the beginning, and GF was designed as a formalism for multilingual rendering of semantic content (Dymetman and al. 2000). XML originated as a format for structuring documents and structured data serialization, but a couple of its descendants, RDF(S) and OWL, developed its potential to formally express the semantics of data and content, serving as the fundaments of the emerging Semantic Web.

Practically any meaning representation format can be converted into GF's abstract syntax, which can then be mapped to different target languages. In particular the OWL language can be seen as a syntactic sugar for a subset of Martin-Löf's type theory so it is trivial to embed it in GF's abstract syntax.

The translation problem defined in terms of an ontology is radically different from the problem of translating plain text from one language to another. Many of the projects in which GF has been used involve precisely this: a meaning representation formalized as GF abstract syntax. Some projects build on previously existing meaning representation and address mathematical proofs (Hallgren and Ranta 2000), software specifications (Beckert & al. 2007), and mathematical exercises (the European project WebALT[6]). Other projects start with semantic modelling work to build meaning representations from scratch, most notably ones for dialogue systems (Perera and Ranta 2007) in the European project TALK[7]. Yet another project, and one closest to web translation, is the multilingual Wiki system presented in (Meza Moreno and Bringert 2008). In this system, users can add and modify reviews of restaurants in three languages (English, Spanish, and Swedish). Any change made in any of the languages gets automatically translated to the other languages.

To take an example, the OWL-to-GF mapping translates OWL's classes to GF's categories and OWL's properties to GF's functions that return propositions. As a running example in this and the next section, we will use the class of integers and the two-place property of being divisible ("x is divisible by y"). The correspondences are as follows:

```
Class(pp:integer ...)
  ⇕
cat integer
ObjectProperty(pp:div
  domain(pp:integer)
  range(pp:integer))
  ⇕
fun div :
  integer ->  integer ->  prop
```

4 Grammar Engineer's Tools

In the GF setting, building a multilingual translation system is equivalent to building a multilingual GF grammar, which in turn consists of two kinds of components:

- a language-independent abstract syntax, giving the semantic model via which translation is performed;

- for each language, a concrete syntax mapping abstract syntax trees to strings in that language.

While abstract syntax construction is an extra task compared to many other kinds of translation methods, it is technically relatively simple, and its cost is moreover amortized as the system is extended to new languages. Concrete syntax construction can be much more demanding in terms of programming skills and linguistic knowledge, due to the complexity of natural languages. This task is where GF claims perhaps the highest advantage over other approaches to special-purpose grammars. The two main assets are:

- Programming language support: GF is a modern functional programming language, with a powerful type system and module system supporting modular and collaborative programming and reuse of code.

- **RGL**, the **GF Resource Grammar Library**, implementing the basic linguistic details of languages: **inflectional morphology** and **syntactic combination functions**.

The RGL covers fifteen languages at the moment, shown in Figure 1; see also Khegai 2006, El Dada and Ranta 2007, Angelov 2008, Ranta 2009a,b, and Enache *et al.* 2010. To give an example of what the library provides, let us first consider the inflectional morphology. It is presented as a set of lexicon-building functions such as, in English,

```
mkV : Str -> V
```

i.e. function `mkV`, which takes a string (`Str`) as its argument and returns a verb (`V`) as its value. The verb is, internally, an inflection table containing all forms of a verb. The function `mkV` derives all these forms from its argument string, which is the infinitive form. It predicts all regular variations: `(mkV "walk")` yields the purely agglutinative forms *walk-walks-walked-walked-walking* whereas `(mkV "cry")` gives *cry-cries-cried-cried-crying*, and so on. For irregular English verbs, RGL gives a three-argument function taking forms such as *sing,sang,sung*, but it also has a fairly complete lexicon of irregular verbs, so that the normal application programmer who builds a lexicon only needs the regular `mkV` function.

Extending a lexicon with domain-specific vocabulary is typically the main part of the work of a concrete syntax author. Considerable work has been put into RGL's inflection functions to make them as "intelligent" as possible and thereby ease the work of the

[6]EDC-22253, webalt.math.helsinki.fi

[7]IST-507802, 2004–2006, www.talk-project.org

users of the library, who don't know the linguistic details of morphology. For instance, even Finnish, whose verbs have hundreds of forms and are conjugated in accordance with around 50 conjugations, has a one-argument function `mkV` that yields the correct inflection table for 90% of Finnish verbs.

As an example of a syntactic combination function of RGL, consider a function for predication with two-place adjectives. This function takes three arguments: a two-place adjective, a subject noun phrase, and a complement noun phrase. It returns a sentence as value:

```
pred : A2 -> NP -> NP -> S
```

This function is available in all languages of RGL, even though the details of sentence formation are vastly different in them. Thus, to give the concrete syntax of the abstract (semantical) predicate `div x y` ("*x* is divisible by *y*"), the English grammarian can write

```
div x y = pred
  (mkA2 "divisible" "by") x y
```

The German grammarian can write

```
div x y = pred
  (mkA2 "teilbar" durch_Prep) x y
```

which, even though superficially using different forms from English, generates a much more complex structure: the complement preposition `durch_Prep` takes care of rendering the argument *y* in the accusative case, and the sentence produced has three forms, as needed in grammatically different positions (*x ist teilbar durch y* in main clauses, *ist x teilbar durch y* after adverbs, and *x durch y teilbar ist* in subordinate clauses).

The syntactic combinations of the RGL have their own abstract syntax, but this abstract syntax is *not* the interlingua of translation: it is only used as a library for implementing the semantic interlingua, which is based on an ontology and abstracts away from syntactic structure. Thus the translation equivalents in a multilingual grammar need not use the same syntactic combinations in different languages. Assume, for the sake of argument, that *x is divisible by y* is expressed in Swedish by the transitive verb construction *y delar x* (literally, "*y* divides *x*"). This can be expressed easily by using the transitive verb predication function of the RGL and switching the subject and object,

```
div x y = pred (mkV2 "dela") y x
```

Thus, even though GF translation is interlingua-based, there is a component of transfer between English and Swedish. But this transfer is performed at compile time. In general, the use of the large-coverage RGL as a library for restricted grammars is called **grammar specialization**. The way GF performs grammar specialization is based on techniques for optimizing functional programming languages, in particular **partial evaluation** (Ranta 2004, 2007). GF also gives a possibility to run-time transfer via semantic actions on abstract syntax trees, but this option has rarely been needed in previous applications, which helps to keep translation systems simple and efficient.

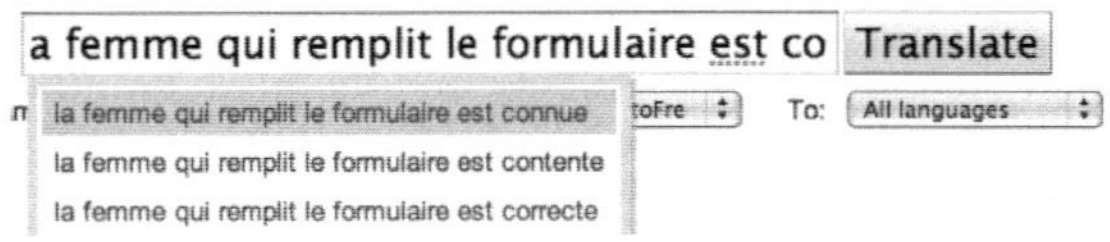

Figure 2: French word prediction in GF parser, suggesting feminine adjectives that agree with the subject *la femme*.

As shown in Figure 1, the RGL is currently available for 15 languages, of which 12 are official languages of the European Union. A similar number of new languages are under construction in this collaborative open-source project. Implementing a new language is an effort of 3–6 person months.

5 Translator's Tools

For the translator's tools, there are three different use cases:

- restricted source
  - production of source in the first place
  - modifying source produced earlier
- unrestricted source

Working with restricted source language recognizable by a GF grammar is straightforward for the translating tool to cope with, except when there is ambiguity in the text. The real challenge is to help the author to keep inside the restricted language. This help is provided by **predictive parsing**, a technique recently developed for GF (Angelov 2009)[8]. Incremental parsing yields **word predictions**, which guide the author in a way similar to the T9 method[9] in mobile phones. The difference from T9 is that GF's word prediction is sensitive to the grammatical context. Thus it does not suggest all existing words, but only those words that are grammatically correct in the context. Figure 2 shows an example of the parser at work. The author has started a sentence as *la femme qui remplit le formulaire est co* ("the woman who fills the form is *co*"), and a menu shows a list of words beginning with *co* that are given in the French grammar and possible in the context at hand; all these words are adjectives in the feminine form. Notice that the very example shown in Figure 2 is one that is difficult for n-gram-based statistical translators: the adjective is so far from the subject with which it agrees that it cannot easily be related to it.

Predictive parsing is a good way to help users produce translatable content in the first place. When modifying the content later, e.g. in a wiki, it may not be optimal, in particular if the text is long. The text can

[8] Parsing in GF is polynomial with an arbitrary exponent in the worst case, but, as shown in Angelov 2009, linear in practice with realistic grammars.

[9] `www.t9.com`

```
Pred known_A (Rel woman_N (Compl fill_V2 form_N))
```
the woman who fills the form is known
la femme qui remplit le formulaire est connue
⟶
```
Pred known_A (Rel man_N (Compl fill_V2 form_N))
```
the **man** who fills the form is known
l' **homme** qui remplit le formulaire est *connu*

Figure 3: Change in one word (boldface) propagated to other words depending on it (italics).

contain parts that depend on each other but are located far apart. For instance, if the word *femme* ("woman") in the previous example is changed to *homme*, the preceding article *la* has to be changed to *l'*, and the adjective has to be changed to the masculine form: thus *connue* ("known") would become *connu*, and so on. Such changes are notoriously difficult even for human authors and translators, and can easily leave a document in an inconsistent state. This is where another utility of the abstract syntax comes in: in the abstract syntax tree, all that is changed is the noun, and the regenerated concrete syntax string automatically obeys all the agreement rules. The process is shown in Figure 3. The one-word change generating the new set of documents can be performed by editing any of the three representations: the tree, the English version, or the French version. This functionality is implemented in the GF **syntax editor** (Khegai & al. 2003).

Restricted languages in the sense of GF are close to **controlled languages**, such as Attempto (Fuchs & al. 2008); the examples shown in this section are actually taken from a GF implementation that generalizes Attempto Controlled English to five languages (Angelov and Ranta 2009). However, unlike typical controlled languages, GF does not require the absence of ambiguity. In fact, when a controlled language is generalized to new languages, lexical ambiguities in particular are hard to avoid.

The predictive parser of GF does not try to resolve ambiguities, but simply returns all alternatives in the parse chart. If the target language has exactly the same ambiguity, it remains hidden in the translation. But if the ambiguity does make a difference in translation, it has to be resolved, and the system has to provide a possibility of manual disambiguation by the user to guarantee high quality.

The translation tool snapshot in Figure 2 is from an actual web-based prototype. It shows a slot in an HTML page, built by using JavaScript via the Google Web Toolkit (Bringert & al. 2009). The translation is performed using GF in a server, which is called via HTTP. Also client-side translators, with similar user interfaces, can be built by converting the whole GF grammar to JavaScript (Meza Moreno and Bringert 2008).

6 The Demo

In the demo, we will show

- how a simple translation system is built and compiled by using the GF grammar compiler and the resource grammar library
- how the translator is integrated in a web page
- how the translator is used in a web browser by means of an integrated incremental parser

A preliminary demo can be seen in `http://grammaticalframework.org:41296`. All the demonstrated tools are available as open-source software from `http://grammaticalframework.org`.

The work reported here is supported by MOLTO (Multilingual On-Line Translation. FP7-ICT-247914).

References

Alshawi, H. (1992). *The Core Language Engine*. Cambridge, Ma: MIT Press.

Angelov, K. (2008). Type-Theoretical Bulgarian Grammar. In B. Nordström and A. Ranta (Eds.), *Advances in Natural Language Processing (GoTAL 2008)*, Volume 5221 of *LNCS/LNAI*, pp. 52–64. URL `http://www.springerlink.com/content/978-3-540-85286-5/`.

Angelov, K. (2009). Incremental Parsing with Parallel Multiple Context-Free Grammars. In *Proceedings of EACL'09, Athens*.

Angelov, K. and A. Ranta (2009). Implementing Controlled Languages in GF. In *Proceedings of CNL-2009, Marettimo*, LNCS. to appear.

Bar-Hillel, Y. (1964). *Language and Information*. Reading, MA: Addison-Wesley.

Beckert, B., R. Hähnle, and P. H. Schmitt (Eds.) (2007). *Verification of Object-Oriented Software: The KeY Approach*. LNCS 4334. Springer-Verlag.

Bender, E. M. and D. Flickinger (2005). Rapid prototyping of scalable grammars: Towards modularity in extensions to a language-independent core. In *Proceedings of the 2nd International Joint Conference on Natural Language Processing IJCNLP-05 (Posters/Demos)*, Jeju Island, Korea. URL `http://faculty.washington.edu/ebender/papers/modules05.pdf`.

Bresnan, J. (Ed.) (1982). *The Mental Representation of Grammatical Relations*. MIT Press.

Bringert, B., K. Angelov, and A. Ranta (2009). Grammatical Framework Web Service. In *Proceedings of EACL'09, Athens*.

Butt, M., H. Dyvik, T. H. King, H. Masuichi, and C. Rohrer (2002). The Parallel Grammar Project. In *COLING 2002, Workshop on Grammar Engineering and Evaluation*, pp. 1–7. URL http://www2.parc.com/isl/groups/nltt/pargram/buttetal-coling02.pdf.

Chandioux, J. (1976). MÉTÉO: un système opérationnel pour la traduction automatique des bulletins météreologiques destinés au grand public. *META 21*, 127–133.

Curry, H. B. (1961). Some logical aspects of grammatical structure. In R. Jakobson (Ed.), *Structure of Language and its Mathematical Aspects: Proceedings of the Twelfth Symposium in Applied Mathematics*, pp. 56–68. American Mathematical Society.

Dada, A. E. and A. Ranta (2007). Implementing an Open Source Arabic Resource Grammar in GF. In M. Mughazy (Ed.), *Perspectives on Arabic Linguistics XX*, pp. 209–232. John Benjamin's.

Dean, M. and G. Schreiber (2004). OWL Web Ontology Language Reference. URL http://www.w3.org/TR/owl-ref/.

Dymetman, M., V. Lux, and A. Ranta (2000). XML and multilingual document authoring: Convergent trends. In *COLING, Saarbrücken, Germany*, pp. 243–249. URL http://www.cs.chalmers.se/~aarne/articles/coling2000.ps.gz.

Enache, R., A. Ranta, and K. Angelov (2010). An Open-Source Computational Grammar for Romanian. In A. Gelbukh (Ed.), *Intelligent Text Processing and Computational Linguistics (CICLing-2010), Iasi, Romania, March 2010, LNCS*, to appear.

Fuchs, N. E., K. Kaljurand, and T. Kuhn (2008). Attempto Controlled English for Knowledge Representation. In C. Baroglio, P. A. Bonatti, J. Małuszyński, M. Marchiori, A. Polleres, and S. Schaffert (Eds.), *Reasoning Web, Fourth International Summer School 2008*, Number 5224 in Lecture Notes in Computer Science, pp. 104–124. Springer.

Hallgren, T. and A. Ranta (2000). An extensible proof text editor. In M. Parigot and A. Voronkov (Eds.), *LPAR-2000*, Volume 1955 of *LNCS/LNAI*, pp. 70–84. Springer. URL http://www.cs.chalmers.se/~aarne/articles/lpar2000.ps.gz.

Harper, R., F. Honsell, and G. Plotkin (1993). A Framework for Defining Logics. *JACM 40*(1), 143–184.

Joshi, A. (1985). Tree-adjoining grammars: How much context-sensitivity is required to provide reasonable structural descriptions. In D. Dowty, L. Karttunen, and A. Zwicky (Eds.), *Natural Language Parsing*, pp. 206–250. Cambridge University Press.

Khegai, J. (2006). GF Parallel Resource Grammars and Russian. In *Coling/ACL 2006*, pp. 475–482.

Khegai, J., B. Nordström, and A. Ranta (2003). Multilingual Syntax Editing in GF. In A. Gelbukh (Ed.), *Intelligent Text Processing and Computational Linguistics (CICLing-2003), Mexico City, February 2003*, Volume 2588 of *LNCS*, pp. 453–464. Springer-Verlag. URL http://www.cs.chalmers.se/~aarne/articles/mexico.ps.gz.

Martin-Löf, P. (1984). *Intuitionistic Type Theory*. Napoli: Bibliopolis.

Meza Moreno, M. S. and B. Bringert (2008). Interactive Multilingual Web Applications with Grammarical Framework. In B. Nordström and A. Ranta (Eds.), *Advances in Natural Language Processing (GoTAL 2008)*, Volume 5221 of *LNCS/LNAI*, pp. 336–347. URL http://www.springerlink.com/content/978-3-540-85286-5/.

Montague, R. (1974). *Formal Philosophy*. New Haven: Yale University Press. Collected papers edited by Richmond Thomason.

Perera, N. and A. Ranta (2007). Dialogue System Localization with the GF Resource Grammar Library. In *SPEECHGRAM 2007: ACL Workshop on Grammar-Based Approaches to Spoken Language Processing, June 29, 2007, Prague*. URL http://www.cs.chalmers.se/~aarne/articles/perera-ranta.pdf.

Pollard, C. and I. Sag (1994). *Head-Driven Phrase Structure Grammar*. University of Chicago Press.

Power, R. and D. Scott (1998). Multilingual authoring using feedback texts. In *COLING-ACL*.

Ranta, A. (1994). *Type Theoretical Grammar*. Oxford University Press.

Ranta, A. (2004). Grammatical Framework: A Type-Theoretical Grammar Formalism. *The Journal of Functional Programming 14(2)*, 145–189. URL http://www.cs.chalmers.se/~aarne/articles/gf-jfp.ps.gz.

Ranta, A. (2009a). Grammars as Software Libraries. In Y. Bertot, G. Huet, J.-J. Lévy, and G. Plotkin (Eds.), *From Semantics to Computer Science*. Cambridge University Press. URL http://www.cs.chalmers.se/~aarne/articles/libraries-kahn.pdf.

Ranta, A. (2009b). The GF Resource Grammar Library. In *Linguistic Issues in Language Technology*, Vol. 2. URL http://elanguage.net/journals/index.php/lilt/article/viewFile/214/158.

Rosetta, M. T. (1994). *Compositional Translation*. Dordrecht: Kluwer.

Shieber, S. M. and Y. Schabes (1990). Synchronous tree-adjoining grammars. In *COLING*, pp. 253–258.

Demonstration of a prototype for a Conversational Companion for reminiscing about images

Yorick Wilks
IHMC, Florida
ywilks@ihmc.us

Roberta Catizone
University of Sheffield, UK
r.catizone@dcs.shef.ac.uk

Alexiei Dingli
University of Malta, Malta
alexiei.dingli@um.edu.mt

Weiwei Cheng
University of Sheffield, UK
w.cheng@dcs.shef.ac.uk

Abstract

This paper describes an initial prototype demonstrator of a Companion, designed as a platform for novel approaches to the following: 1) The use of Information Extraction (IE) techniques to extract the content of incoming dialogue utterances after an Automatic Speech Recognition (ASR) phase, 2) The conversion of the input to Resource Descriptor Format (RDF) to allow the generation of new facts from existing ones, under the control of a Dialogue Manger (DM), that also has access to stored knowledge and to open knowledge accessed in real time from the web, all in RDF form, 3) A DM implemented as a stack and network virtual machine that models mixed initiative in dialogue control, and 4) A tuned dialogue act detector based on corpus evidence. The prototype platform was evaluated, and we describe this briefly; it is also designed to support more extensive forms of emotion detection carried by both speech and lexical content, as well as extended forms of machine learning.

1. Introduction

This demonstrator Senior Companion (SC) was built during the initial phase of the Companions project and aims to change the way we think about the relationships of people to computers and the internet by developing a virtual conversational 'Companion that will be an agent or 'presence' that stays with the user for long periods of time, developing a relationship and 'knowing its owners' preferences and wishes. The Companion communicates with the user primarily through speech, but also using other technologies such as touch screens and sensors.

This paper describes the functionality and system modules of the Senior Companion, one of two initial prototypes built in the first two years of the project. The SC provides a multimodal interface for eliciting, retrieving and inferring personal information from elderly users by means of conversation about their photographs. The Companion, through conversation, elicits life memories and reminiscences, often prompted by discussion of their photographs; the aim is that the Companion should come to know a great deal about its user, their tastes, likes, dislikes, emotional reactions etc, through long periods of conversation. It is assumed that most life information will soon be stored on the internet (as in the Memories for Life project: http://www.memoriesforlife.org/) and we have linked the SC directly to photo inventories in Facebook (see below). The overall aim of the SC project (not yet achieved) is to produce a coherent life narrative for its user from conversations about personal photos, although its short-term goals, reported here, are to assist, amuse and entertain the user.

The technical content of the project is to use a number of types of machine learning (ML) to achieve these ends in original ways, initially using a methodology developed in earlier research: first, by means of an Information Extraction (IE) approach to deriving content from user input utterances; secondly, using a training method for attaching Dialogue Acts to these utterance and, lastly, using a specific type of dialogue manager (DM) that uses Dialogue Action Forms (DAF) to determine the context of any utterance. A stack of these DAFs is the virtual machine that models the ongoing dialogue by means of shared user and Companion initiative and generates appropriate responses. In this description of the demo, we shall:

- describe the current SC prototype's functionality;
- set out its architecture and modules, focusing on the Natural Language Understanding module and the Dialogue Manager.

A mini-version of the demo running in real time can be seen at: URL

Proceedings of the ACL 2010 System Demonstrations, pages 72–77,
Uppsala, Sweden, 13 July 2010.

http://www.youtube.com/watch?v=-Xx5hgjD-Mw

2. The Senior Companion System

The Senior Companion prototype (Wilks, 2010) was designed to make a rapid advance in the first two years of the project so as to be basis for a second round of prototypes embodying more advanced ML. This strategy was deliberately chosen to avoid a well-known problem with experimental AI systems: that a whole project is spent in design so that a prototype never emerges until the very end, but which is then never fully evaluated and, most importantly, nothing is ever built on the experience obtained in its construction. The central function of the SC is engaging the user in discussion about their photographs: where and when they were taken, details about the people in them and their relationship to the user and each other.

Once a photo is loaded, it is processed with face recognition software to identify any faces in it. The recognition software, OpenCV, provides positional information by identifying the face coordinates and this information is exploited in the Dialogue Manager by making explicit reference to the position of people in the photograph (the person on the left, right, center, etc.) as well as recognizing when there are groups of people. The system discusses properties of the photo as well as properties and relationships of the people in the photos.

The news reading feature adds an interesting accompaniment to the photo domain and demonstrates the ability of the system to handle more than one kind of application at a time, and news has, of course, an unconstrained vocabulary. The following is a fairly typical example of its current capacity, depending of course on the images loaded, and comes from the middle part of a sample dialogue generated by the system when discussing a group photo from a vacation in Zanzibar, and after the system had already stored, from an earlier conversation, that the user has a daughter Zoe (using researchers' children to avoid any problems):

SC: What is your relationship to the doctor?
User: There is no relationship.
SC: Please tell me how you know the doctor
U: Uh, he's a friend.
SC: How old was the doctor when this photo was taken?
U: I'm not sure but I think about 30.
SC: How do you know Octavia?
U: She's my daughter.
SC: Aha! I see. Octavia's sister is Zoe.
SC: How old was your daughter Octavia when this photo was taken?
U: Octavia was 19 years old.
SC: What was the occasion of this photo?
U: This was another family holiday.
SC: Where was this photo taken?
U: This photo was taken in Tanzania.
SC: have you ever been to Zanzibar?
U: Yes, I have.
SC: Great place, I hope you saw the beaches. When was this photo taken?
U: last year.

It is a key feature of the SC that it can make simple inferences from family relationships it already knows (e.g. that daughters of the same parent are siblings) and that it can access real-time information about places to show that it has some knowledge of what is being talked about, in this case the beaches on Zanzibar, and how this is done is discussed below. This real time access to unconstrained place information on the internet is an attempt to break out of classic AI systems that only know the budget of facts they have been primed with.

This basic system provides the components for future development of the SC, as well as its main use as a device to generate more conversation data for machine learning research in the future. Key features of the SC are listed below followed by a description of the system architecture and modules. The SC:

- Contains a visually appealing multimodal interface with a character avatar to mediate the system's functionality to the user.
- Interacts with the user using multiple modalities – speech and touch.
- Includes face detection software for identifying the position of faces in the photos.
- Accepts pre-annotated (XML) photo inventories as a means for creating richer dialogues more quickly.
- Engages in conversation with the user about topics within the photo domain: when and where the photo was taken, discussion of the people in the photo including their relationships to the user.
- Reads news from three categories: politics, business and sports.

- Tells jokes taken from an internet-based joke website.
- Retains all user input for reference in repeat user sessions, in addition to the knowledge base that has been updated by the Dialogue Manager on the basis of what was said.
- Contains a fully integrated Knowledge Base for maintaining user information including:
    - Ontological information which is exploited by the Dialogue Manager and provides domain-specific relations between fundamental concepts.
    - A mechanism for storing information in a triple store (Subject-Predicate-Object) - the RDF Semantic Web format - for handling unexpected user input that falls outside of the photo domain, e.g. arbitrary locations in which photos might have been taken.
    - A reasoning module for reasoning over the Knowledge Base and world knowledge obtained in RDF format from the internet; the SC is thus a primitive Semantic Web device (see refernce8, 2008)
- Contains basic photo management capability allowing the user, in conversation, to select photos as well as display a set of photos with a particular feature.

Figure 1: The Senior Companion Interface

3. System Architecture

In this section we will review the components of the SC architecture. As can be seen from Figure 2, the architecture contains three abstract level components – Connectors, Input Handlers and Application Services –together with the Dialogue Manager and the Natural Language Understander (NLU).

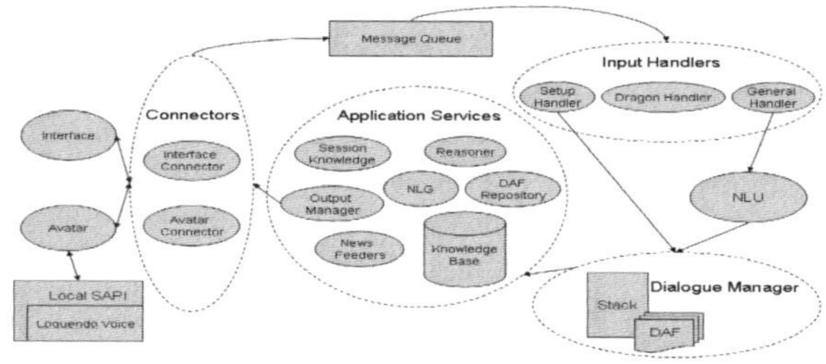

Figure 2: Senior Companion system architecture

Connectors form a communication bridge between the core system and external applications. The external application refers to any modules or systems which provide a specific set of functionalities that might be changed in the future. There is one connector for each external application. It hides the underlying complex communication protocol details and provides a general interface for the main system to use. This abstraction decouples the connection of external and internal modules and makes changing and adding new external modules easier. At this moment, there are two connectors in the system – Napier Interface Connector and CrazyTalk Avatar Connector. Both of them are using network sockets to send/receive messages.

Input Handlers are a set of modules for processing messages according to message types. Each handler deals with a category of messages where categories are coarse-grained and could include one or more message types. The handlers separate the code handling inputs into different places and make the code easier to locate and change. Three handlers have been implemented in the Senior Companion system – Setup Handler, Dragon Events Handler and General Handler. The Setup Handler is responsible for loading the photo annotations if any, performing face detection if no annotation file is associated with the photo and checking the Knowledge Base in case the photo being processed has been discussed in earlier sessions. Dragon Event Handler deals with dragon speech recognition commands sent from the interface while the General Handler processes user utterances and photo change events of the interface.

Application Services are a group of internal modules which provide interfaces for the Dialogue Action Forms (DAF) to use. It has an easy-to-use high-level interface for general DAF designers to code associated tests and actions as well as a low level interface for advanced DAFs. It also provides the communication link between DAFs and the internal system and enables DAFs to access system functionalities. Following is a brief summary of modules grouped into Application Services.

News Feeders are a set of RSS Feeders for fetching news from the internet. Three different news feeders have been implemented for fetching news from BBC website Sports, Politics and Business channels. There is also a Jokes Feeder to fetch Jokes from internet in a similar way. During the conversation, the user can request news about particular topics and the SC simply reads the news downloaded through the feeds.

The DAF Repository is a list of DAFs loaded from files generated by the DAF Editor.

The Natural Language Generation (NLG) module is responsible for randomly selecting a system utterance from a template. An optional variable can be passed when calling methods on this module. The variable will be used to replace special symbols in the text template if applicable.

Session Knowledge is the place where global information for a particular running session is stored. For example, the name of the user who is running the session, the list of photos being discussed in this session and the list of user utterances etc.

The Knowledge Base is the data store of persistent knowledge. It is implemented as an RDF triplestore using a Jena implementation. The triplestore API is a layer built upon a traditional relational database. The application can save/retrieve information as RDF triples rather than table records. The structure of knowledge represented in RDF triples is discussed later.

The Reasoner is used to perform inference on existing knowledge in the Knowledge Base (see example in next section).

The Output Manager deals with sending messages to external applications. It has been implemented in a publisher/subscriber fashion. There are three different channels in the system: the text channel, the interface command channel and the avatar command channel. Those channels could be subscribed to by any connectors and handled respectively.

4. Dialogue understanding and inference

Every utterance is passed through the Natural Language Understanding (NLU) module for processing. This module uses a set of well-established natural language processing tools such as those found in the GATE (Cunningham, et al., 1997) system. The basic processes carried out by GATE are: tokenizing, sentence splitting, POS tagging, parsing and Named Entity Recognition. These components have been further enhanced for the SC system by adding 1) new and improved gazetteers including family relations and 2) accompanying extraction rules .The Named Entity (NE) recognizer is a key part of the NLU module and recognizes the significant entities required to process dialogue in the photo domain: PERSON NAMES, LOCATION NAMES, FAMILY RELATIONS and DATES. Although GATE recognizes basic entities, more complex entities are not handled. Apart from the gazetteers mentioned earlier and the hundreds of extraction rules already present in GATE, about 20 new extraction rules using the JAPE rule language were also developed for the SC module. These included rules which identify complex dates, family relationships, negations and other information related to the SC domain. The following is an example of a simple rule used to identify relationship in utterances such as “Mary is my sister”:

```
Macro: RELATIONSHIP_IDENTIFIER
(
({To-
ken.category=="PRP$"}|{Token.category=="PR
P"}|{Lookup.majorType=="person_first"}):pers
on2
({Token.string=="is"})
({Token.string=="my"}):person1
({Lookup.minorType=="Relationship"}):relation
ship)
```

Using this rule with the example mentioned earlier, the rule interprets person1 as referring to the speaker so, if the name of the user speaking is John (which was known from previous conversations), it is utilized. Person 2 is then the name of the person mentioned, i.e. Mary. This name is recognised by using the gazetteers we have in the system (which contain about 40,000 first names). The relationship is once again identified using the almost 800 unique relationships added to the gazetteer. With this information, the NLU module identifies Information Extraction patterns in the dialogue that represent significant content with respect to a user's life and photos.

The information obtained (such as Mary=sister-of John) is passed to the Dialogue Manager (DM) and then stored in the knowledge base (KB). The DM filters what to include and exclude from the KB. Given, in the example above, that Mary is the sister of John, the NLU knows that sister is a relationship between two people and is a key relationship. However, the NLU also discovers syntactical information such as the fact the both Mary and John are nouns. Even though this information is important, it is too low level to be of any use by the SC with respect to the user, i.e. the user is not interested in the parts-of-speech of a word. Thus, this information is discarded by the DM and not stored in the KB. The NLU module also identifies a Dialogue Act Tag for each user utterance based on the DAMSL set of DA tags and prior work done jointly with the University of Albany (Webb et al., 2008).

The KB is a long-term store of information which makes it possible for the SC to retrieve information stored between different sessions. The information can be accessed anytime it is needed by simply invoking the relevant calls. The structure of the data in the database is an RDF triple, and the KB is more commonly referred to as a triple store. In mathematical terms, a triple store is nothing more than a large database of interconnected graphs. Each triple is made up of a subject, a predicate and an object. So, if we took the previous example, Mary sister-of John; Mary would be the subject, sister-of would be the predicate and John would be the object. The inference engine is an important part of the system because it allows us to discover new facts beyond what is elicited from the conversation with the user.

Uncle Inference Rule:
(?a sisterOf ?b),
(?x sonOf ?a),
(?b gender male) -> (?b uncleOf ?x)

Triples:
(Mary sisterOf John)
(Tom sonOf Mary)

Triples produced automatically by ANNIE (the semantic tagger):
(John gender male)

Inference:
(Mary sisterOf John)
(Tom sonOf Mary)
(John gender male)
->
(John uncleOf Tom)

This kind of inference is already used by the SC and we have about 50 inference rules aimed at producing new data on the relationships domain. This combination of triple store, inference engine and inference rules makes a system which is weak but powerful enough to mimic human reasoning in this domain and thus simulate basic intelligence in the SC. For our prototype, we are using the JENA Semantic Web Framework for the inference engine together with a MySQL database as the knowledge base. However, this system of family relationships is not enough to cover all the possible topics which can crop up during a conversation and, in such circumstances, the DM switches to an open-world model and instructs the NLU to seek further information online.

5. The Hybrid-world approach

When the DM requests further information on a particular topic, the NLU first checks with the KB whether the topic is about something known. At this stage, we have to keep in mind that any topic requested by the DM should be already in the KB since it was preprocessed by the NLU when it was mentioned in the utterance. So, if the user informs the system that the photograph was taken in Paris, (in response to a system question asking where the photo was taken), the utterance is first processed by the NLU which discovers that "Paris" is a location using its semantic tagger ANNIE (A Nearly New Information Extraction engine). The semantic tagger makes use of gazetteers and IE rules in order to accomplish this task. It also goes through the KB and retrieves any triples related to "Paris". Inference is then performed on this data and the new information generated by this process is stored back in the KB.

Once the type of information is identified, the NLU can use various predefined strategies: In the case of LOCATIONS, one of the strategies used is to seek for information in Wiki-Travel or Virtual Tourists. The system already knows how to query these sites and interpret their output by using predefined wrappers. This is then used to extract relevant information from the mentioned sites webpages by sending an online query to these sites and storing the information retrieved in the triple-store. This information is then used by the DM to generate a reply. In the previous example, the system manages to extract the best sightseeing spots in Paris. The NLU would then store in the KB triples such as [Paris, sightseeing, Eiffel Tower] and the DM with the help of the NLG would ask the user "I've heard that the X is a very famous spot. Have you seen it while you were there?" Obviously in this case, X would be replaced by the "Eiffel Tower".

On the other hand, if the topic requested by the DM is unknown, or the semantic tagger is not capable of understanding the semantic category, the system uses a normal search engine (and this is what we call "hybrid-world": the move outside the world the system already knows). A query containing the unknown term in context is sent to standard engines and the top pages are retrieved. These pages are then processed using ANNIE and their tagged attributes are analyzed. The standard attributes returned by ANNIE include information about Dialogue Acts, Polarity (i.e. whether a sentence has positive, negative or neutral connotations), Named Entities, Semantic Categories (such as dates and currency), etc. The system then filters the information collected by using more generic patterns and generates a reply from the resultant information. ANNIE's polarity methods have been shown to be an adequate implementation of the general word-based polarity methods pioneered by Wiebe and her colleagues (see e.g. Akkaya et al., 2009).

6. Evaluation

The notion of companionship is not yet one with any agreed evaluation strategy or metric, though developing one is part of the main project itself. Again, there are established measures for the assessment of dialogue programs but they have all been developed for standard task-based dialogues and the SC is not of that type: there is no specific task either in reminiscing conversations, nor in the elicitation of the content of photos, that can be assessed in standard ways, since there is no clear point at which an informal dialogue need stop, having been completed. Conventional dialogue evaluations often use measures like "stickiness" to determine how much a user will stay with or stick with a dialogue system and not leave it, presumably because they are disappointed or find it lacking in some feature. But it is hard to separate that feature out from a task rapidly and effectively completed, where stickiness would be low not high. Traum (Traum et al., 2004) has developed a methodology for dialogue evaluation based on "appropriateness" of responses and the Companions project has developed a model of evaluation for the SC based on that (Benyon et al., 2008).

Acknowledgement

This work was funded by the Companions project (2006-2009) sponsored by the European Commission as part of the Information Society Technologies (IST) programme under EC grant number IST-FP6-034434.

References

David Benyon, Prem Hansen and Nick Webb, 2008. Evaluating Human-Computer Conversation in Companions. In: *Proc.4th International Workshop on Human-Computer Conversation*, Bellagio, Italy.

Cem Akkaya, Jan Wiebe, and Rada Mihalcea,. 2009. Subjectivity Word Sense Disambiguation, In: *EMNLP 2009.*

Hamish Cunningham, Kevin Humphreys, Robert Gaizauskas, and Yorick Wilks, 1997. GATE -- a TIPSTER based General Architecture for Text Engineering. In: *Proceedings of the TIPSTER Text Program (Phase III) 6 Month Workshop*. Morgan Kaufmann, CA.

David Traum, Susan Robinson, and Jens Stephan. 2004. Evaluation of multi-party virtual reality dialogue interaction, In: *Proceedings of Fourth International Conference on Language Resources and Evaluation (LREC 2004)*, pp.1699-1702

Yorick Wilks (ed.) 2010. *Artificial Companions in Society: scientific, economic, psychological and philosophical perspectives.* John Benjamins: Amsterdam.

It Makes Sense: A Wide-Coverage Word Sense Disambiguation System for Free Text

Zhi Zhong and **Hwee Tou Ng**
Department of Computer Science
National University of Singapore
13 Computing Drive
Singapore 117417
{zhongzhi, nght}@comp.nus.edu.sg

Abstract

Word sense disambiguation (WSD) systems based on supervised learning achieved the best performance in SensEval and SemEval workshops. However, there are few publicly available open source WSD systems. This limits the use of WSD in other applications, especially for researchers whose research interests are not in WSD.

In this paper, we present IMS, a supervised English all-words WSD system. The flexible framework of IMS allows users to integrate different preprocessing tools, additional features, and different classifiers. By default, we use linear support vector machines as the classifier with multiple knowledge-based features. In our implementation, IMS achieves state-of-the-art results on several SensEval and SemEval tasks.

1 Introduction

Word sense disambiguation (WSD) refers to the task of identifying the correct sense of an ambiguous word in a given context. As a fundamental task in natural language processing (NLP), WSD can benefit applications such as machine translation (Chan et al., 2007a; Carpuat and Wu, 2007) and information retrieval (Stokoe et al., 2003).

In previous SensEval workshops, the supervised learning approach has proven to be the most successful WSD approach (Palmer et al., 2001; Snyder and Palmer, 2004; Pradhan et al., 2007). In the most recent SemEval-2007 English all-words tasks, most of the top systems were based on supervised learning methods. These systems used a set of knowledge sources drawn from sense-annotated data, and achieved significant improvements over the baselines.

However, developing such a system requires much effort. As a result, very few open source WSD systems are publicly available – the only other publicly available WSD system that we are aware of is SenseLearner (Mihalcea and Csomai, 2005). Therefore, for applications which employ WSD as a component, researchers can only make use of some baselines or unsupervised methods. An open source supervised WSD system will promote the use of WSD in other applications.

In this paper, we present an English all-words WSD system, IMS (It Makes Sense), built using a supervised learning approach. IMS is a Java implementation, which provides an extensible and flexible platform for researchers interested in using a WSD component. Users can choose different tools to perform preprocessing, such as trying out various features in the feature extraction step, and applying different machine learning methods or toolkits in the classification step. Following Lee and Ng (2002), we adopt support vector machines (SVM) as the classifier and integrate multiple knowledge sources including parts-of-speech (POS), surrounding words, and local collocations as features. We also provide classification models trained with examples collected from parallel texts, SEMCOR (Miller et al., 1994), and the DSO corpus (Ng and Lee, 1996).

A previous implementation of the IMS system, NUS-PT (Chan et al., 2007b), participated in SemEval-2007 English all-words tasks and ranked first and second in the coarse-grained and fine-grained task, respectively. Our current IMS implementation achieves competitive accuracies on several SensEval/SemEval English lexical-sample and all-words tasks.

The remainder of this paper is organized as follows. Section 2 gives the system description, which introduces the system framework and the details of the implementation. In Section 3, we present the evaluation results of IMS on SensE-

Proceedings of the ACL 2010 System Demonstrations, pages 78–83,
Uppsala, Sweden, 13 July 2010. ©2010 Association for Computational Linguistics

val/SemEval English tasks. Finally, we conclude in Section 4.

2 System Description

In this section, we first outline the IMS system, and introduce the default preprocessing tools, the feature types, and the machine learning method used in our implementation. Then we briefly explain the collection of training data for content words.

2.1 System Architecture

Figure 1 shows the system architecture of IMS. The system accepts any input text. For each content word w (noun, verb, adjective, or adverb) in the input text, IMS disambiguates the sense of w and outputs a list of the senses of w, where each sense s_i is assigned a probability according to the likelihood of s_i appearing in that context. The sense inventory used is based on WordNet (Miller, 1990) version 1.7.1.

IMS consists of three independent modules: preprocessing, feature and instance extraction, and classification. Knowledge sources are generated from input texts in the preprocessing step. With these knowledge sources, instances together with their features are extracted in the instance and feature extraction step. Then we train one classification model for each word type. The model will be used to classify test instances of the corresponding word type.

2.1.1 Preprocessing

Preprocessing is the step to convert input texts into formatted information. Users can integrate different tools in this step. These tools are applied on the input texts to extract knowledge sources such as sentence boundaries, part-of-speech tags, etc. The extracted knowledge sources are stored for use in the later steps.

In IMS, preprocessing is carried out in four steps:

- Detect the sentence boundaries in a raw input text with a sentence splitter.
- Tokenize the split sentences with a tokenizer.
- Assign POS tags to all tokens with a POS tagger.
- Find the lemma form of each token with a lemmatizer.

By default, the sentence splitter and POS tagger in the OpenNLP toolkit[1] are used for sentence splitting and POS tagging. A Java version of Penn TreeBank tokenizer[2] is applied in tokenization. JWNL[3], a Java API for accessing the WordNet (Miller, 1990) thesaurus, is used to find the lemma form of each token.

2.1.2 Feature and Instance Extraction

After gathering the formatted information in the preprocessing step, we use an instance extractor together with a list of feature extractors to extract the instances and their associated features.

Previous research has found that combining multiple knowledge sources achieves high WSD accuracy (Ng and Lee, 1996; Lee and Ng, 2002; Decadt et al., 2004). In IMS, we follow Lee and Ng (2002) and combine three knowledge sources for all content word types[4]:

- *POS Tags of Surrounding Words* We use the POS tags of three words to the left and three words to the right of the target ambiguous word, and the target word itself. The POS tag feature cannot cross sentence boundary, which means all the associated surrounding words should be in the same sentence as the target word. If a word crosses sentence boundary, the corresponding POS tag value will be assigned as *null*.

  For example, suppose we want to disambiguate the word *interest* in a POS-tagged sentence "My/PRP$ brother/NN has/VBZ always/RB taken/VBN a/DT keen/JJ interest/NN in/IN my/PRP$ work/NN ./.". The 7 POS tag features for this instance are *<VBN, DT, JJ, NN, IN, PRP$, NN>*.

- *Surrounding Words* Surrounding words features include all the individual words in the surrounding context of an ambiguous word w. The surrounding words can be in the current sentence or immediately adjacent sentences.

  However, we remove the words that are in a list of stop words. Words that contain no alphabetic characters, such as punctuation

[1] http://opennlp.sourceforge.net/
[2] http://www.cis.upenn.edu/~treebank/tokenizer.sed
[3] http://jwordnet.sourceforge.net/
[4] Syntactic relations are omitted for efficiency reason.

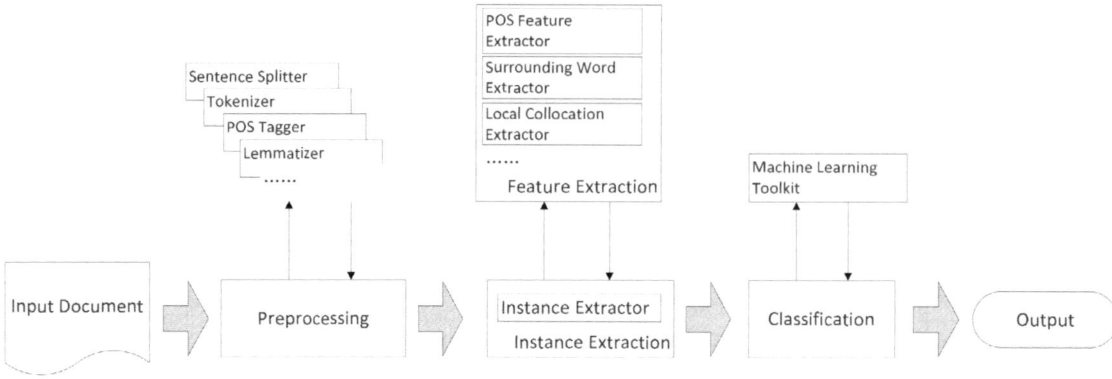

Figure 1: IMS system architecture

symbols and numbers, are also discarded. The remaining words are converted to their lemma forms in lower case. Each lemma is considered as one feature. The feature value is set to be 1 if the corresponding lemma occurs in the surrounding context of w, 0 otherwise.

For example, suppose there is a set of surrounding words features $\{$*account*, *economy*, *rate*, *take*$\}$ in the training data set of the word *interest*. For a test instance of *interest* in the sentence "My brother has always taken a keen interest in my work .", the surrounding word feature vector will be $<$0, 0, 0, 1$>$.

- *Local Collocations* We use 11 local collocations features including: $C_{-2,-2}$, $C_{-1,-1}$, $C_{1,1}$, $C_{2,2}$, $C_{-2,-1}$, $C_{-1,1}$, $C_{1,2}$, $C_{-3,-1}$, $C_{-2,1}$, $C_{-1,2}$, and $C_{1,3}$, where $C_{i,j}$ refers to an ordered sequence of words in the same sentence of w. Offsets i and j denote the starting and ending positions of the sequence relative to w, where a negative (positive) offset refers to a word to the left (right) of w.

  For example, suppose in the training data set, the word *interest* has a set of local collocations $\{$*"account ."*, *"of all"*, *"in my"*, *"to be"*$\}$ for $C_{1,2}$. For a test instance of *interest* in the sentence "My brother has always taken a keen interest in my work .", the value of feature $C_{1,2}$ will be *"in my"*.

As shown in Figure 1, we implement one feature extractor for each feature type. The IMS software package is organized in such a way that users can easily specify their own feature set by implementing more feature extractors to exploit new features.

2.1.3 Classification

In IMS, the classifier trains a model for each word type which has training data during the training process. The instances collected in the previous step are converted to the format expected by the machine learning toolkit in use. Thus, the classification step is separate from the feature extraction step. We use LIBLINEAR[5] (Fan et al., 2008) as the default classifier of IMS, with a linear kernel and all the parameters set to their default values. Accordingly, we implement an interface to convert the instances into the LIBLINEAR feature vector format.

The utilization of other machine learning software can be achieved by implementing the corresponding module interfaces to them. For instance, IMS provides module interfaces to the WEKA machine learning toolkit (Witten and Frank, 2005), LIBSVM[6], and MaxEnt[7].

The trained classification models will be applied to the test instances of the corresponding word types in the testing process. If a test instance word type is not seen during training, we will output its predefined default sense, i.e., the WordNet first sense, as the answer. Furthermore, if a word type has neither training data nor predefined default sense, we will output "U", which stands for the missing sense, as the answer.

[5] `http://www.bwaldvogel.de/liblinear-java/`

[6] `http://www.csie.ntu.edu.tw/~cjlin/libsvm/`

[7] `http://maxent.sourceforge.net/`

2.2 The Training Data Set for All-Words Tasks

Once we have a supervised WSD system, for the users who only need WSD as a component in their applications, it is also important to provide them the classification models. The performance of a supervised WSD system greatly depends on the size of the sense-annotated training data used. To overcome the lack of sense-annotated training examples, besides the training instances from the widely used sense-annotated corpus SEMCOR (Miller et al., 1994) and DSO corpus (Ng and Lee, 1996), we also follow the approach described in Chan and Ng (2005) to extract more training examples from parallel texts.

The process of extracting training examples from parallel texts is as follows:

- Collect a set of sentence-aligned parallel texts. In our case, we use six English-Chinese parallel corpora: Hong Kong Hansards, Hong Kong News, Hong Kong Laws, Sinorama, Xinhua News, and the English translation of Chinese Treebank. They are all available from the Linguistic Data Consortium (LDC).
- Perform tokenization on the English texts with the Penn TreeBank tokenizer.
- Perform Chinese word segmentation on the Chinese texts with the Chinese word segmentation method proposed by Low et al. (2005).
- Perform word alignment on the parallel texts using the GIZA++ software (Och and Ney, 2000).
- Assign Chinese translations to each sense of an English word w.
- Pick the occurrences of w which are aligned to its chosen Chinese translations in the word alignment output of GIZA++.
- Identify the senses of the selected occurrences of w by referring to their aligned Chinese translations.

Finally, the English side of these selected occurrences together with their assigned senses are used as training data.

We only extract training examples from parallel texts for the top 60% most frequently occurring polysemous content words in Brown Corpus (BC), which includes 730 nouns, 190 verbs, and 326 adjectives. For each of the top 60% nouns and adjectives, we gather a maximum of 1,000 training examples from parallel texts. For each of the top 60% verbs, we extract not more than 500 examples from parallel texts, as well as up to 500 examples from the DSO corpus. We also make use of the sense-annotated examples from SEMCOR as part of our training data for all nouns, verbs, adjectives, and 28 most frequently occurring adverbs in BC.

POS	noun	verb	adj	adv
# of types	11,445	4,705	5,129	28

Table 1: Statistics of the word types which have training data for WordNet 1.7.1 sense inventory

The frequencies of word types which we have training instances for WordNet sense inventory version 1.7.1 are listed in Table 1. We generated classification models with the IMS system for over 21,000 word types which we have training data. On average, each word type has 38 training instances. The total size of the models is about 200 megabytes.

3 Evaluation

In our experiments, we evaluate our IMS system on SensEval and SemEval tasks, the benchmark data sets for WSD. The evaluation on both lexical-sample and all-words tasks measures the accuracy of our IMS system as well as the quality of the training data we have collected.

3.1 English Lexical-Sample Tasks

	SensEval-2	SensEval-3
IMS	**65.3%**	72.6%
Rank 1 System	64.2%	**72.9%**
Rank 2 System	63.8%	72.6%
MFS	47.6%	55.2%

Table 2: WSD accuracies on SensEval lexical-sample tasks

In SensEval English lexical-sample tasks, both the training and test data sets are provided. A common baseline for lexical-sample task is to select the most frequent sense (MFS) in the training data as the answer.

We evaluate IMS on the SensEval-2 and SensEval-3 English lexical-sample tasks. Table 2 compares the performance of our system to the top two systems that participated in the above tasks (Yarowsky et al., 2001; Mihalcea and Moldovan, 2001; Mihalcea et al., 2004). Evaluation results show that IMS achieves significantly better accuracies than the MFS baseline. Comparing to the top participating systems, IMS achieves comparable results.

3.2 English All-Words Tasks

In SensEval and SemEval English all-words tasks, no training data are provided. Therefore, the MFS baseline is no longer suitable for all-words tasks. Because the order of senses in WordNet is based on the frequency of senses in SEMCOR, the WordNet first sense (WNs1) baseline always assigns the first sense in WordNet as the answer. We will use it as the baseline in all-words tasks.

Using the training data collected with the method described in Section 2.2, we apply our system on the SensEval-2, SensEval-3, and SemEval-2007 English all-words tasks. Similarly, we also compare the performance of our system to the top two systems that participated in the above tasks (Palmer et al., 2001; Snyder and Palmer, 2004; Pradhan et al., 2007). The evaluation results are shown in Table 3. IMS easily beats the WNs1 baseline. It ranks first in SensEval-3 English fine-grained all-words task and SemEval-2007 English coarse-grained all-words task, and is also competitive in the remaining tasks. It is worth noting that because of the small test data set in SemEval-2007 English fine-grained all-words task, the differences between IMS and the best participating systems are not statistically significant.

Overall, IMS achieves good WSD accuracies on both all-words and lexical-sample tasks. The performance of IMS shows that it is a state-of-the-art WSD system.

4 Conclusion

This paper presents IMS, an English all-words WSD system. The goal of IMS is to provide a flexible platform for supervised WSD, as well as an all-words WSD component with good performance for other applications.

The framework of IMS allows us to integrate different preprocessing tools to generate knowledge sources. Users can implement various feature types and different machine learning methods or toolkits according to their requirements. By default, the IMS system implements three kinds of feature types and uses a linear kernel SVM as the classifier. Our evaluation on English lexical-sample tasks proves the strength of our system. With this system, we also provide a large number of classification models trained with the sense-annotated training examples from SEMCOR, DSO corpus, and 6 parallel corpora, for all content words. Evaluation on English all-words tasks shows that IMS with these models achieves state-of-the-art WSD accuracies compared to the top participating systems.

As a Java-based system, IMS is platform independent. The source code of IMS and the classification models can be found on the homepage: `http://nlp.comp.nus.edu.sg/software` and are available for research, non-commercial use.

Acknowledgments

This research is done for CSIDM Project No. CSIDM-200804 partially funded by a grant from the National Research Foundation (NRF) administered by the Media Development Authority (MDA) of Singapore.

References

Marine Carpuat and Dekai Wu. 2007. Improving statistical machine translation using word sense disambiguation. In *Proceedings of the 2007 Joint Conference on Empirical Methods in Natural Language Processing and Computational Natural Language Learning (EMNLP-CoNLL)*, pages 61–72, Prague, Czech Republic.

Yee Seng Chan and Hwee Tou Ng. 2005. Scaling up word sense disambiguation via parallel texts. In *Proceedings of the 20th National Conference on Artificial Intelligence (AAAI)*, pages 1037–1042, Pittsburgh, Pennsylvania, USA.

Yee Seng Chan, Hwee Tou Ng, and David Chiang. 2007a. Word sense disambiguation improves statistical machine translation. In *Proceedings of the 45th Annual Meeting of the Association for Computational Linguistics (ACL)*, pages 33–40, Prague, Czech Republic.

Yee Seng Chan, Hwee Tou Ng, and Zhi Zhong. 2007b. NUS-PT: Exploiting parallel texts for word sense disambiguation in the English all-words tasks. In *Proceedings of the Fourth International Workshop on Semantic Evaluations (SemEval-2007)*, pages 253–256, Prague, Czech Republic.

Bart Decadt, Veronique Hoste, and Walter Daelemans. 2004. GAMBL, genetic algorithm optimization of memory-based WSD. In *Proceedings of the Third*

	SensEval-2 Fine-grained	SensEval-3 Fine-grained	SemEval-2007 Fine-grained	SemEval-2007 Coarse-grained
IMS	68.2%	**67.6%**	58.3%	**82.6%**
Rank 1 System	**69.0%**	65.2%	**59.1%**	82.5%
Rank 2 System	63.6%	64.6%	58.7%	81.6%
WNs1	61.9%	62.4%	51.4%	78.9%

Table 3: WSD accuracies on SensEval/SemEval all-words tasks

International Workshop on Evaluating Word Sense Disambiguation Systems (SensEval-3), pages 108–112, Barcelona, Spain.

Rong-En Fan, Kai-Wei Chang, Cho-Jui Hsieh, Xiang-Rui Wang, and Chih-Jen Lin. 2008. LIBLINEAR: A library for large linear classification. *Journal of Machine Learning Research*, 9:1871–1874.

Yoong Keok Lee and Hwee Tou Ng. 2002. An empirical evaluation of knowledge sources and learning algorithms for word sense disambiguation. In *Proceedings of the 2002 Conference on Empirical Methods in Natural Language Processing (EMNLP)*, pages 41–48, Philadelphia, Pennsylvania, USA.

Jin Kiat Low, Hwee Tou Ng, and Wenyuan Guo. 2005. A maximum entropy approach to Chinese word segmentation. In *Proceedings of the Fourth SIGHAN Workshop on Chinese Language Processing*, pages 161–164, Jeju Island, Korea.

Rada Mihalcea and Andras Csomai. 2005. Sense-Learner: Word sense disambiguation for all words in unrestricted text. In *Proceedings of the 43rd Annual Meeting of the Association for Computational Linguistics (ACL) Interactive Poster and Demonstration Sessions*, pages 53–56, Ann Arbor, Michigan, USA.

Rada Mihalcea and Dan Moldovan. 2001. Pattern learning and active feature selection for word sense disambiguation. In *Proceedings of the Second International Workshop on Evaluating Word Sense Disambiguation Systems (SensEval-2)*, pages 127–130, Toulouse, France.

Rada Mihalcea, Timothy Chklovski, and Adam Kilgarriff. 2004. The SensEval-3 English lexical sample task. In *Proceedings of the Third International Workshop on Evaluating Word Sense Disambiguation Systems (SensEval-3)*, pages 25–28, Barcelona, Spain.

George Miller, Martin Chodorow, Shari Landes, Claudia Leacock, and Robert Thomas. 1994. Using a semantic concordance for sense identification. In *Proceedings of ARPA Human Language Technology Workshop*, pages 240–243, Morristown, New Jersey, USA.

George Miller. 1990. Wordnet: An on-line lexical database. *International Journal of Lexicography*, 3(4):235–312.

Hwee Tou Ng and Hian Beng Lee. 1996. Integrating multiple knowledge sources to disambiguate word sense: An exemplar-based approach. In *Proceedings of the 34th Annual Meeting of the Association for Computational Linguistics (ACL)*, pages 40–47, Santa Cruz, California, USA.

Franz Josef Och and Hermann Ney. 2000. Improved statistical alignment models. In *Proceedings of the 38th Annual Meeting of the Association for Computational Linguistics (ACL)*, pages 440–447, Hong Kong.

Martha Palmer, Christiane Fellbaum, Scott Cotton, Lauren Delfs, and Hoa Trang Dang. 2001. English tasks: All-words and verb lexical sample. In *Proceedings of the Second International Workshop on Evaluating Word Sense Disambiguation Systems (SensEval-2)*, pages 21–24, Toulouse, France.

Sameer Pradhan, Edward Loper, Dmitriy Dligach, and Martha Palmer. 2007. SemEval-2007 task-17: English lexical sample, SRL and all words. In *Proceedings of the Fourth International Workshop on Semantic Evaluations (SemEval-2007)*, pages 87–92, Prague, Czech Republic.

Benjamin Snyder and Martha Palmer. 2004. The English all-words task. In *Proceedings of the Third International Workshop on Evaluating Word Sense Disambiguation Systems (SensEval-3)*, pages 41–43, Barcelona, Spain.

Christopher Stokoe, Michael P. Oakes, and John Tait. 2003. Word sense disambiguation in information retrieval revisited. In *Proceedings of the Twenty-Sixth Annual International ACM SIGIR Conference on Research and Development in Information Retrieval (SIGIR)*, pages 159–166, Toronto, Canada.

Ian H. Witten and Eibe Frank. 2005. *Data Mining: Practical Machine Learning Tools and Techniques*. Morgan Kaufmann, San Francisco, 2nd edition.

David Yarowsky, Radu Florian, Siviu Cucerzan, and Charles Schafer. 2001. The Johns Hopkins SensEval-2 system description. In *Proceedings of the Second International Workshop on Evaluating Word Sense Disambiguation Systems (SensEval-2)*, pages 163–166, Toulouse, France.

Author Index